Presented to ....

....

From ....

Date ....

Also by Maulana Wahiduddin Khan

The Moral Vision
Islam As It Is
Religion and Science
A Treasury of the Qur'an
Woman in Islamic Shari'ah
Islam: Creator of the Modern Age
Words of the Prophet Muhammad
Islam: The Voice of Human Nature
An Islamic Treasury of Virtues
Woman Between Islam and Western Society
Islam and the Modern Man
Muhammad: A Prophet for All Humanity
Muhammad: The Ideal Character
Islam and Peace
Principles of Islam
The Call of the Qur'an
The Qur'an: An Abiding Wonder
The Quran For All Humanity
The Good Life
The Way to Find God
The Teachings of Islam
The Garden of Paradise
The Fire of Hell
Indian Muslims
Tabligh Movement
Man Know Thyself
Polygamy and Islam
Hijab in Islam
Concerning Divorce
Uniform Civil-Code
Introducing Islam
God Arises

Introducing

Islam

A Simple Introduction to Islam

Maulana Wahiduddin Khan

Goodword
B·O·O·K·S

Translated by Farida Khanam

First published 1999
Reprinted 2013
© Goodword Books 2013

Goodword Books
1, Nizamuddin West Market, New Delhi-110 013
Mob. +91-8588822672
Tel. 9111-4182-7083, 4652-1511
email: info@goodwordbooks.com
www.goodwordbooks.com

Islamic Vision Ltd.
434 Coventry Road, Small Heath
Birmingham B10 0UG, U.K.
Tel. 121-773-0137
Fax: 121-766-8577
e-mail: info@ipci-iv.co.uk, www.islamicvision.co.uk

IB Publisher Inc.
81 Bloomingdale Rd, Hicksville
NY 11801, USA
Tel. 516-933-1000
Fax: 516-933-1200
Toll Free: 1-888-560-3222
email: info@ibpublisher.com, www.ibpublisher.com

Printed in India

Contents

7

Introduction

For some time now there has been a need for an introduction to Islam, presented in simple and concise language, which might provide children with fundamental religious instruction and also be useful to adults who want to understand the teachings of Islam.

By the grace of God a book of this nature has now been compiled. It consists of five parts, the names of which are as follows: The Way to Find God, The Teachings of Islam, The Good Life, The Garden of Paradise and The Fire of Hell.

The Way to Find God

The title of the first part is self-explanatory. Man requires guidance in his search for God. The universe provides man with such guidance in visual form. The whole universe seems to be beckoning man to join it in its inexorable progress towards the Lord. So dazzling is the sun's radiance that it seems to wish to convey a message to man, but cannot do so before setting. Trees extend their branches. Rivers flow on in their pulsating motion. All these things and many others have something to say, but men pass them by without ever realizing what that something is. All celestial heights and terrestrial panoramas seem to join in a massive yet silent congregation, which addresses itself to man visually, though never audibly.

But is the universe really no more than a vast museum of inarticulate masterpieces? Not at all. Everything in it bears a divine message, communicated in the language of eternity. So immersed is man in other worldly affairs, however, that he fails to hear this silent message.

The Prophet's role is to put this divine message into words that we can understand. He demonstrates the kind of life that God expects man and the whole of creation to lead.

The Qur'an—the word of God in Arabic—is the foundation of this inspired path. The *sunnah*—the life and teachings of the Prophet Muhammad, (on whom be peace and God's blessings), collected in several volumes—provides clarification of the Holy Book. Whoever seriously wishes to understand Islam should study these books, for they are the authentic source of God's religion. Here is a comprehensive course for those who do not have time to study them all:

1. The Holy Qur'an
2. *Sirat ibn Kathir* (Biography of the Prophet) by Ibn Kathir
3. Hadith, *Mishkat al-Masabih*
4. *Hayat as-Sahabah* (Life of the Companions) by Muhammad Yusuf Kandhalvi

These are well-known and easily—obtainable

books. Though originally written in Arabic, they have been translated and published in several languages. They can be acquired and read in the language of one's choice.

This essay has been prepared with a general and fundamental understanding of the divine way in mind. If it imbues the reader with a desire to study religion in more detail and delve deeper into reality, then it will have been worthwhile.

The Teaching of Islam

Islam is not just a system; it is a means of becoming acquainted with the Lord of the Universe. A study of Islam should move one as proximity to God does. To understand Islam, one should read a book which does not just deal with creeds but also explains how one should establish one's relationship with the Creator; which does not just describe conditions which will prevail in the next life, but also instills one with fear and apprehension about what is to be one's lot in the hereafter; which penetrates to the spirit of worship and does not merely concern itself with the way it should be performed; which does not simply explain one's obligations to one's fellow-men, but also encourages one to fulfill these obligations and refrain from injustice.

This is an attempt to provide such a treatise on Islam. May God accept it.

The Good Life

This is the third paer of this book. It comprises excerpts from the Qur'an, arranged in a special sequence under relevant headings. No interpretation or commentary has been added. It provides an introduction to Islam which is derived directly from the original revealed source.

The name of this book is taken from a verse of the Qur'an, the full text of which is:

> Be they men or women those, who believe and do what is right We shall surely endow with a good life: We shall reward them according to their noblest actions (16:97).

The meaning of the "good life" mentioned in this verse is clear from the phrase "according to their noblest actions". A good life is a life of good actions. The commentator of the Qur'an, ad-Dahhak, has defined it as "being content with an honest living and serving God in one's life." This is the meaning that the Companions of the Prophet and their followers generally inferred from the phrase.

To believe in God and implement His commandments is to qualify oneself for His succour. God bestows multiple blessings on a person who lives a life of faith and righteousness. He enables him to experience the joy of closeness to God in his worship; to settle day-to-day problems in a divinely-inspired manner; to deal with friends and foe in an equally honest-to-God way. God guides him on the straight path. He always seeks God's pleasure and nothing can turn him away from this aim.

The Qur'an has given a clear exposition of the theoretical and practical nature of the good life. The verses which have been selected describe various fundamental aspects of this life in the Qur'an's inimitable style. These passages thus provide both a description of the good life and an authentic example of how it should be lived.

The Garden of Paradise

God has created an ideal world called paradise. It is a world of everlasting joy and bliss. No turmoil or pain mars its delight. One is never beset there by anguish or calamity. It is a trouble-free world of infinite blessings, where one will experience neither death, boredom nor grief.

The search for such an ideal world is an instinctive urge in man. Everybody is searching for an invisible paradise; but none is able to find a paradise of such infinite blessings in the present finite world. God has reserved it for the next world.

None can earn paradise automatically; only those who perform heavenly actions on earth will be deserving of it. God has divided our lives into two parts: a short period on earth, and the rest in the hereafter. This world is for action. The next world is for reaping the rewards of our actions.

Man is free to do as he wishes on earth, but his free

16

will is no more than a test. He should treat it as such. He should not revel in his power. Those who are not deluded by their temporary power, and never lose sight of their true position, will be accommodated in paradise. Those who rebel on the basis of their worldly power will abide in hell.

All real power in this world belongs to God alone. He is the Lord of all things. No one can escape from His control for an instant. Those who recognise this fact will submit to God of their own accord. They are the ones who are worthy of paradise. Those who deny this fact and proceed in whatever direction their impulse takes them, are offenders in God's sight. They will have no share in the blessings of the life-hereafter.

The Fire of Hell

The most powerful motivating force in our lives is fear. Consciously or subconsciously, everyone's actions are the result of some kind of fear. It could be of financial ruin, worldly disgrace, a powerful enemy, or some superior power. Each and every person functions because of some real or imaginary fear.

Yet there is no substance to the actions which people perform on the basis of such fear, for there is no substance to the objects which they fear. The only fear which is of any value is fear of God, and sincere actions can result only from true awe and apprehension of one God.

God has created man: He controls the vast universe and has complete power over man's destiny. Anyone who truly believes this will certainly fear God. But there is more to the matter than this: God will raise us up after death and will judge us according to our words and deeds on earth. We are responsible to Him for our actions.

One has to think seriously about life when one considers it from this point of view. If we keep in mind our eternal destiny, we shall then have no choice but to submit to the Lord who created us, and who will judge us after death.

We must do our utmost to protect ourselves and others from the torment of hell fire. God's Prophets taught man the reality of life. According to their teachings the real issue facing us in life is how to avoid God's punishment in the next world. We must prepare ourselves for meeting God and must exhort others to do the same. As Muslims, this is the basic task that lies before us. Other things that we desire in life can be ours only if we perform this fundamental task.

Wahiduddin Khan
October, 1980
The Islamic Centre,
New Delhi

PART ONE
The Way to Find God

Man's Quest

Much as we long for a perfect world, we are compelled to live in an imperfect one. Our happiness is always short-lived and our every success is, in some way, eventually a failure. The aspirations that we cherish in the early days of our lives are shattered as we begin to age. Just as we begin to take root on earth, disaster, old age and death overtake us.

How enchanting the flowers are, but they blossom only to wither. How delicate the sun's radiance, but it shines for only a short while before being covered in darkness. Miraculous though man's existence is, no miracle can save him from death. Everything in this world shall perish. Although this world is inexpressibly beautiful and meaningful, all its virtues are bound to fade. All mundane things have a dark side to them. How, one may ask, could a God who is Himself perfect, be satisfied with the creation of an intrinsically imperfect world? The absolute cannot abide in the non-absolute. This world must be inconclusive. Another world must follow to compensate for the inadequacies of the present one.

There is no doubt about the transitory nature of this world. It came into existence at a specific time some twenty million years ago. Its Creator must have existed eternally, for only an infinite Creator could have fashioned a finite world. If God had not always existed, then this transitory world could never have come into being. The very existence of an ephemeral universe shows that there must be an eternal Creator. If the Creator had not existed eternally, He could never have existed at all and, if there had been no Creator, there would have been no creation either.

If we assert that the world was created on a certain date, then this means that there must have been a Creator before that date. If we go on to assert that this Creator was Himself created on some previous date, however, then our claim can have no meaning. The Creator cannot himself have been created; He always was. In His infiniteness He has created a finite world. His existence, and that of all mortal creatures, is dependent upon His immortality.

Since God is immortal, He must also be absolute, for absoluteness is the greatest attribute of immortality. The one cannot be found without the other.

This world is a manifestation of God's attributes, but its shortcomings and limitations show the manifestation to be incomplete. A complete manifestation of a perfect and infinite God would itself be perfect and infinite. Another world must be awaiting us. This incomplete manifestation of God's attributes requires a sequel for its fulfillment.

Paradise is that eternal world of God in which His

attributes will appear in all their perfection. It will be free of all the defects we experience in the world about us. Paradise is evidence of God's absolute power to make beauty perpetual and joy boundless in a world of everlasting peace and contentment.

Everyone is seeking some unseen fulfillment. Everyone seeks a perfect world, but this has always eluded man. Yet it is quite natural that he should continue to strive, for the universe in which he lives testifies to the existence of one, infinite God. The emergence of a world of infinite blessings is just as likely as the existence of the present transitional world. How can an inherently infinite Creator be satisfied with a finite manifestation of His attributes? God, Who created all things from nought, can surely endow creation with perpetuity. This second creation is no more difficult than the first.

Immortality is God's unique quality, in which He has no partner. Immortality signifies the highest possible perfection to which only God can attain. No one can today imagine the wonderful nature of that paradise which is a manifestation of God's immortality: that beauty which will never fade; that joy which will never end; that life, the continuity of which will never be interrupted; that world where all our hopes and desires will be fulfilled. No one will wish to part for even a moment from this wondrously delightful paradise, no matter how many millions of years have passed.

Man is always searching for a world of everlasting content. This quest is quite correct and in accordance with human nature; but our dreams cannot come true in this world, for here, there cannot be an eternally perfect order. The resources needed for such a world are lacking. The Prophet taught that God has made this world one of trial and tribulation, not one of reward and retribution. The world is full of things which put man to the test, whereas the factors required for a life of everlasting delight and repose will be forthcoming only in the next world. Death divides these two worlds. Death marks the completion of the trial of man and his entrance into the world of eternity.

If one wishes one's dreams to come true, one should not try to construct a heaven on earth. One should rather try to succeed in the trial of life, accepting the role of God's true servant, adopting the life pattern of the Prophet and restricting one's freedom to the limits which God has laid down. The dreams of those who succeed in the trial of life will be fulfilled in the next world. Those who fail will find nothing but woe awaiting them there.

What is Truth?

There is only one straight line from one point to another; so there can only be one path leading a person to God. This is the true path. The question is: what does truth consist of and how can it be found?

Fortunately for us, there are not several truths to choose from. There is only one truth for us to accept. This solitary truth consists of the teachings of Muhammad, the Prophet of God, on whom be peace and God's blessings. Anyone who earnestly seeks the truth will find that no exacting choices have to be made. The choice is between truth and falsehood; there are no two truths to choose from.[1]

For at least five thousand years philosophers have searched in vain for truth. Their tedious investigations have only exposed their inability to provide conclusive answers. Philosophy seeks truth by means of rational contemplation, not realizing that knowledge of the entire cosmos—something beyond the range of the limited human intellect—is a pre-requisite for genuine gnosis. The philosopher can never attain to cosmic knowledge, so that neither can he conceive of an accurate idea of reality.

---

1. Qur'an, 10:32.

Science has never claimed to be in a position to explain the truth. It only looks into matters which can be repeatedly proved experimentally. Science discusses the chemistry of flowers, but not their fragrance, for the chemical parts of a flower can be analysed; its odour cannot. Science has itself restricted its scope, making it clear that it will deal only with partial truth and is in no position to expound on universal realities.

Some spiritual adepts claim, or their followers believe, that they know all about truth, and can communicate absolute information concerning it, but their belief is groundless. They claim to have reached the truth by means of spiritual disciplines. The so-called spiritual disciplines are in fact of a physical nature, and spiritual discovery by means of physical discipline is an unfeasible proposition in itself. Secondly, no spiritual adept is free of the limitations to which all men are subject. The obstacles which prevent others from reaching a full understanding of truth also block his path. No self-discipline can enable man to transcend these natural limitations and convey to him a knowledge of absolute truth.

So the stage is left to the Prophet. A prophet is a human being who asserts that God has chosen him and revealed true knowledge to him for the purpose of conveying it to others. Intrinsically, this is the only plausible claim so far, for only God, who is eternal and omniscient, can have actual knowledge of truth. God's divinity itself is proof of His all-pervading knowledge of reality. The claim of one who asserts that he has received knowledge of truth from God is worthy of consideration.

Here the question arises of there having been not just one prophet. There are many divine scriptures and many prophets have been sent to the world; which of them should be followed? A person who is really sincere in his search for truth, however, will have no trouble in finding the answer to this question. There is no doubt that in the past God has raised many individuals to the status of prophethood, but one can judge an event only by virtue of its historical credibility and only one prophet possesses credentials which make his prophethood a historical certainty rather than just a belief. Of all those who have claimed prophethood, only Muhammad, on whom be peace and God's blessings, can be said to have achieved full historical credibility. Everything about him is established historical fact. We are just as well informed about the Prophet of Islam as we are about any contemporary person, or even more so. Apart from him, all prophets are legendary figures. No complete historical record of them exists, nor are the scriptures they left preserved in their original state. Only the life of Muhammad ﷺ has been completely chronicled. The book which was handed over to people as the inspired word of God is also present in its original form. So, looking at the matter rationally, there can only be one answer to the question. "What is truth?" From a practical as well as a theoretical point of view, we should accept the only realistic answer there is. We should not try to select a solution from a wide range of alternatives.

This truth is the word of God and the word of God is immutable. God's commandments never change, either with respect to man or the rest of creation. The terrestrial and celestial orders have not altered despite the passing of billions of years. The principles which govern vegetation and water in one location are equally applicable in another. That is the way with God's commandments to man also: they are the same now as they were thousands of years ago. That which applies to one nation applies with equal force to all.

Some factors in life, such as transport or architecture, are continually being altered, but truth always remains the same. Truth is attached to that side of human nature which never changes. The truth is concerned with matters like whom one should accept as one's Creator and Master; whom one should worship; whom one should love and whom one should fear; according to what criteria one should assess success and failure; what the purpose of one's existence is and the focal point of one's emotions; according to what code of conduct one should deal with people. Truth deals with matters which are not affected by time and place. Everyone, at all times and in all places is confronted by these questions. Just as God is one and everlasting, so the truth is also one and will always remain so.

A Danger Warning

What is the reality of life? Normally people do not like to think of such things. For them, there is one life—that of the world—and they try to live it in as prestigious and comfortable a way as possible, for afterwards, neither man, nor anything that concerns him, will remain. Some do think about this matter, but only on a philosophical level. They seek a theoretical explanation of the world. Such explanations are interesting from a philosophical point of view, but they are of no basic value to man. Theoretical discussions about whether a cosmic spirit keeps the whole universe revolving for its own fulfillment, or whether everything is part of some sublime being, do not raise any personal issues for man. Some have a religious answer to the question, but their solution is also of no import to man. Some religions hold that the son of God was crucified in atonement for man's sins; others see life as a mysterious, recurring cycle, with man repeatedly being born and dying; some claim that man will be rewarded and punished in this world. These are the creeds of which most religions are made.

All such solutions to the problems of life differ from one another considerably but in so much as none of them raises any serious personal issue for man, they

28

are all the same. They are either explanations of events or a means of providing us with some sort of spiritual satisfaction. They do not issue us with any warning or stir us into any action.

But the answer provided by the Prophet Muhammad is of an entirely different nature. Whereas the other answers do not raise any critical issue for man, the answer provided by the Prophet places every individual in a precarious position from which the next step leads either to an awesome abyss of destruction or to a world of eternal bliss. It requires every man to take a serious view of his situation—even more so than a traveller in the night whose torch reveals a black snake slithering menacingly in front of him.

The message taught by Muhammad, may God's peace and blessings be upon him, contains a greater warning for all mankind. He taught that after this world a vaster world is awaiting us, where every person will be judged and then punished or rewarded according to his deeds. The props which man relies on in this world will not support him there, for there will be no trading, no friendship and no acceptable intercession.[1]

The warning which the Prophet delivered to mankind makes his existence a matter of personal importance to everyone. Everyone's fate, according to his teachings, hangs in the balance. Either one can believe in his message and follow his guidance, thus preparing oneself for

1. Qur'an, 2:254

everlasting paradise, or one can ignore his teachings, thus resigning oneself to eternal hellfire.

There are two things which make this matter even more worthy of our attention. Firstly, the arguments of those who have expounded other theories on this matter have been very dubious. Those who consider material aggrandisement to be all that is worthwhile in life have no proof for their theory; their ideas are based on superficial attractions. Those who speak in philosophical terms have only analogies to offer as evidence. They themselves do not have full faith in what they say, so how can others be expected to accept their theories?

Then there are those who speak with reference to the prophets and scriptures. Basically their platform is solid, but the prophets and books to which they refer belong to an age-long past. We have no reliable historical information regarding them at our disposal. Even though the original source of these religions is sound, we still cannot rely on their teachings as they are at present. The criterion with which to judge the past is history, and history does not verify the authenticity of their dogmas.

With the Prophet Muhammad, however, the case is quite different. On the one hand, his prophetic credentials stand up to any scrutiny. He was the epitome of everything a prophet should be. There is no doubt about his prophethood; it is an established historical fact which no one can deny.

The facts of the Holy Prophet's life and teachings have also been carefully preserved; their historical credibility cannot be contested. The Qur'an exists in its revealed form. The Holy Prophet's words and actions are recorded in book-form, so one has no difficulty in establishing exactly what he said and did in his life.

The Prophet warned us that we are confronted with a reality which we can never change; we have no choice but to face it. Death and suicide only transfer us to another world; they do not obliterate us altogether. The Creator has established an eternal scheme for success and failure which no one can alter or opt out of. We have to choose between heaven and hell; we have no other choice.

If the meteorological department forecasts a hurricane, it is telling us about an impending disaster in which those affected will have no say in the matter; another power will control events. One can either escape or expose oneself to destruction. So, when the earthquake of the Last day occurs there will be no path to safety save that which the Prophet of Islam has laid down. We ignore that path at our own peril.

The Teachings
of the Prophet

God's religion is one religion. It is that one religion which has always been revealed to prophets, but man, in his carelessness, has always marred or altered the true way. The Prophet Muhammad revived the divine religion and presented it in scriptural form for posterity. His religion is the true religion until the end of time. It is the only way to achieve closeness to God and salvation in the afterlife.

He taught that God is One; He has no partner. He created all things and has complete control over the universe. We should serve Him and submit to Him alone. In Him should we repose our hopes and to Him should we pray. Though He cannot be seen, he is so close to us that he hears and answers us when we call upon Him. There is no greater sin than to consider that He could have any counterpart or equal.

There is no intermediary between God and man. By remembering God, a person establishes direct contact with Him; there is no need for any go-between. No one will be able to intercede before God in the Hereafter either. He will decide everyone's case according to His own knowledge; no one will be able to influence His judgement. God is not accountable to

32

anyone for His decisions. All His judgements are based on wisdom and justice; He is not influenced by intercession and proximity.

Worship of God is much more than just superficial rituals; it is total submission. If one worships God, then one devotes oneself entirely to one's Lord, fearing Him, loving Him, having hopes in Him, and concentrating on Him alone. Worship of God is total self-surrender; it is much more than occasional observance of mere formalities.

When dealing with others, we should always bear in mind that God is watching over us. He will deal with us as we have dealt with others. So, in order to avoid recrimination when our actions are weighed up on the divine scales of justice, it is essential that we avoid evils such as cruelty, dishonesty, pride, antagonism, jealousy, selfishness and callousness. If one fears God, one will not treat His creatures with disdain, for those who mistreat God's creatures should not expect kindness from the Creator; only those who have treated others well deserve good treatment from Him.

The Prophet taught that the only acceptable life is one of total obedience to God. The basic principles of this life are forms of subservience as laid down in the Qur'an, and God's Prophet has demonstrated them practically in his life. The only life pleasing to God, then, is one which follows the guidance of the Qur'an and the example set by the Holy Prophet.

The religion which the Prophet left us guides us in

every walk of life; everyone should proceed in accordance with the scheme with which he has provided us. This scheme is based on certain tenets on which the whole of the Islamic life is based.

Firstly, there is the testimony: "There is no one worthy of being served save God, and Muhammad is His messenger." This declaration marks man's exit from one arena and his entry into another—his departure from all that is un-Islamic and his inclusion in the ranks of Islam. Secondly, prayer, that is worship five times a day in the manner of the Prophet. Thirdly, fasting, a test of patience and endurance annually performed during the month of Ramadan. Fourthly *zakat,* the setting aside of a fixed portion of one's income for the poor. Fifthly, pilgrimage, a visit to the House of God at least once in a lifetime, if one has the means. When one fulfills these five conditions, one becomes part of the prophetically established Islamic brotherhood.

Life can be lived in either of two ways; it can be founded either on the Hereafter or on the world. In the former case, the Prophet's guidance is accepted and a person forms his beliefs and arranges his life according to his instructions. In the latter case a person guides himself, letting his own intellect dictate the way he thinks and acts. The first person can be called a God-worshipper, while the second is a self-worshipper.

There are several parts to the credo based on

prophetic guidance: belief in God, the angels, the scriptures, the prophets, the resurrection of man and life after death, heaven and hell, as well as recognition of God as the overriding Lord and Sovereign. If one bases one's life on these tenets of faith, then one has truly submitted oneself to God. All one's efforts in the world become oriented towards the Hereafter. One's worship, sacrifices, life and death are all dedicated to God and His prophets.

The self-guided life, on the other hand, is a free and unprincipled one. One who lives such a life is unconcerned about the nature of reality. He believes what he wants to; he passes his time in whatever way his intellect and desires direct him; his efforts all centre on worldly gain; he develops into the sort of person he wishes to be, rather than what God and His prophets would like to see.

People who adhere to the religion of some previous prophet can only be counted as God's true servants if they believe in the Prophet of Islam. Belief in him is in no way incompatible with adherence to their own religion in its most complete and perfect possible form. Those who deny his prophethood are proving by their actions that all they follow is a religion of conventional norms and prejudices, to which they have attached a prophet's name. Those who follow a religion simply because it is their national one can never discover the divine religion which the prophet brought. The veil of their prejudices will never allow them to see the truth which God has revealed to the last of His prophets.

Those who really believe in God and His prophets recognize the religion of the Prophet of Islam as their own. They receive it with enthusiasm as one does a long-lost belonging.

Towards Death

Death will overtake everybody; no one can escape from it. But death is not the same for everyone. Some have made God their goal in life; they speak and keep silence for His sake alone; their attention is focused entirely on the after-life. Death is for them the end of a long terrestial journey towards their Lord.

Others have forgotten their Lord; they do not do things for God's sake; they are travelling away from their Lord. They are like rebels who roam at large for a few days, and then death seizes them and brings them to justice.

Death is not the same for both types of people as it might seem. For one, death is to partake of the Lord's hospitality; for the other, it is to be cast into His dungeon. For one, death is the gate to paradise; for the other it will be the day when he is thrown into hell's raging fire, to burn there forever as a punishment for his rebelliousness.

Believers have a different attitude to death from unbelievers. They are concerned with what comes in the wake of death; they focus their attention on gaining an honorable position in the life after death. Unbelievers, on the other hand, are caught up on worldly affairs. Their ultimate ambition is worldly honour and prestige. Under present circumstances, those who have consolidated their position on earth seem to be successful, but death will shatter this facade. It will become clear that those who seemed to have no base in the world were in fact standing on the most solid of foundations, while the position of those who had reached a high status in the world will be exposed as false. Death will obliterate everything; afterwards only that which has some worth in the after-life will remain. We are obsessed with the world which meets our eyes. We fail to pay attention to the call of truth. If we were to see the next life with our worldly vision, we would immediately submit to God. We would realize that if we do not submit to Him today, we will have to do so in the future world, when submission will profit no one.

A Final Word

A city clock-tower informs people of the correct time. People set their watches according to it. Nobody bothers about who the engineers and mechanics who constructed the clock-tower were, or where the parts that they used were produced. The fact that it keeps good time is enough to attract everybody. God's religion is much the same sort of clock-tower, constructed for man's guidance; yet people fail to look at it and find their way by it.

There can only be one reason for this; people are serious in wanting to know the time, but not the word of God. God's religion is connected with the next life, while a clock-tower is a thing of this world. The clock has an important part to play in the realization of their worldly ambitions. They recognize its importance. But they have no ambitions for the future life, and no regard for the importance of something which guides man to eternal success.

True submission to God does not mean just acknowledging His existence. It involves total attachment to Him. It is an inward state with an outward form. Discovery of God is an event of incomparable impact which can never remain hidden. If God's truth has been revealed to someone, it will always be apparent. One so favoured will desire those around him to bear witness to the fact that he has answered the call of God, set aside the idols of worldly gain and expediency, and devoted himself entirely to God. If one claims inner faith, but does not express it, one can only be looking at faith as a convenience. Anyone who puts worldly interests before God cannot ever discover Him. Preoccupation with worldly priorities and prejudices are the very opposite of true submission to God, and two such conflicting states can never merge in one soul.

PART TWO

The Teachings of Islam

The Oneness of God

Say: "He is God, the One, the eternally besought of all. He begets not, nor was He begotten. And there is none comparable to Him" (112:1-4).

All that is in heaven and earth gives glory to God. He is the Mighty, the Wise. His is the kingdom of the heavens and the earth. He ordains life and death and has power over all things. He is the First and Last, the Visible and the Unseen. He has knowledge of all things (57:1-3), and he that renounces idol-worship and puts his faith in God shall grasp a firm handle that will never break.

Allah: there is no God but Him, the Living, the Eternal One. Neither drowsiness nor sleep overtakes Him. His is what the heavens and the earth contain. Who can intercede with Him except by His permission? He knows what is before and behind men. They can grasp only that part of His knowledge which He wills. His throne is as vast as the heavens and the earth, and the preservation of both does not weary him. He is the Sublime, the Tremendous. God hears all and knows all.

God is the Patron of the faithful. He leads them from darkness to the light. As for the unbelievers, their patrons are false Gods, who lead them from light to darkness. They are the heirs of Hell and shall abide in it for ever (2:255-257). Yet there shall be no compulsion in religion. True guidance is never imposed by force.

All Praise is Due to God

A tree is unaware of its own extraordinary significance. A flower does not realize what a delicate and exquisite masterpiece it really is. A bird is oblivious to its own breathtaking beauty. Though all things in this world are classic specimens of the most exquisite art, they never come to know themselves as such.

For whom, then, is this beautiful and gracious display? It is all for man's benefit. Man is the only being in the known universe who can perceive beauty in a thing and appreciate its excellence. God has created exquisite works of art in worldly form and enabled man to apprehend them. He has given man a tongue to express his wonder at and veneration of God's stupendous feats of creation. What he utters is praise, or admiration of God. It is a tribute of the most sublime sentiments, expressed in human words and offered to God.

Praise means being moved at the sight of God's craftsmanship and spontaneously expressing one's realization of His perfection. "God, all praise is due to You. You are chaste and exalted. God, count me among the believers, and raise me not up blind like those who failed to acknowledge your perfection or perceive Your beauty." Praise is constant remembrance of God in this manner, in Arabic or any other language.

The Angels

Amongst the multitudes of beings created by God in His omnipotence are creatures of great luminosity called angels. They are divine servants of impeccable loyalty who convey God's commands throughout the length and breadth of the universe, attending to the workings of His immeasurable kingdom under His all-seeing eye. Their numbers perforce are legion.

The cosmic machine must run with flawless and never-ending consistency. The earth, moon, sun and stars must revolve in their pre-ordained orbits for all eternity. God has willed this to be so, and His angels are the divine instruments through which he ensures the perfect functioning of the universe.

From time immemorial a water cycle of awesome complexity has continued to support life in its myriad forms. Trees and plants of tremendous diversity emerge from the earth at every instant. A whole host of creatures from Man right down to the humblest insect are born and provided for every day. How is it then that such a great multiplicity of events—all of them extremely complex—can take place contemporaneously?

The Prophets in their wisdom have taught that this is all part of a divine order which the Almighty controls through invisible angels acting as His intermediaries. It is they who carry out His commandments and communicate His word to the prophets. They preserve a record of man's actions by means of which God decides which individuals and which nations shall be rewarded or punished. It is the angels who take possession of the human soul at the moment of death, and it is they who will sound the last trumpet which shall throw the whole universe into disarray. It is then that the righteous shall dwell forever in Paradise, while the sinful shall be cast down into hell-fire and eternal damnation.

God's Prophets

When a machine is produced it is accompanied by a set of instructions for its use. An engineer is also commissioned to give a practical demonstration of how the machine functions. Man is an even more intricately designed but animate machine. When he is born, he suddenly finds himself in a world where no mountain bears an inscription answering questions concerning the nature of the world, or explaining how he should live on earth. No educational institution produces experts who know the secret of life or who can provide man with practical guidance.

To satisfy this need felt by man, God sent His prophets to the world, every one of whom brought with him the word of God. In the scriptures revealed to them, God has explained the reality of life to man, and has made it clear what man should and should not do. They showed man what sentiments and ideas he should adopt; how he should remember his Lord; how he should live with his fellows, what he should associate himself with and disassociate himself from. The prophets' lives are a practical demonstration of how a person should live a God-fearing life.

God has given everyone the power to distinguish between right and wrong. He has also placed countless signs in space and on earth from which man can learn. Moreover, His revelations have been set down in human language and several of His servants chosen from amongst mankind as prophets, so that there should be no doubt as to the true path.

Termination of Prophethood

The Arabian Prophet, may God's peace and blessings descend upon him, was the last of God's messengers. No other prophet will now come to the world.

All of God's prophets have taught one and the same religion. They spoke in different languages, but the religion they expounded was one. Since the followers of previous prophets were unable to preserve the prophetic teachings in their original form, messengers of God used to appear frequently in order to revitalize the true religion, and refresh people's memories of it. The Prophet Muhammad for his part initiated a revolutionary process which ensured the preservation of religion in its original form and obviated the necessity for other prophets to follow him by preserving the Book of God intact, in its original form.

God's final Prophet imparted to the true religion a stability which it had never had before. His own life was exemplary, as has been reliably recorded. It is noteworthy, too, that the community that developed after the Prophet continued to demonstrate Islamic practices, like prayer in a practicable and imitable form. People of every subsequent age have found this religion exactly as it was when God's messenger preached it.

The preservation and continuity of religion are now ensured without prophets coming to the world. God's Book and the Prophet's Sunnah are now serving the same purpose which it had taken a succession of prophets to accomplish. It is the duty of their followers to carry on their mission.

The Resurrection

Every night is followed by day. That which is concealed in night's darkness can be clearly seen in the light of day. In the same manner, this ephemeral world will be followed by an eternal one, in which all realities will become as clear as daylight. In this world, one is able to conceal evil under a false exterior. Some are eloquent enough to clothe their falsity in a righteous garb, whilst others mask their inner impurity under refulgent exteriors. The true character of every individual is shrouded in darkness, but the resurrection will tear all veils asunder and lay bare the reality.

What a startling revelation this will be! All men will be where they really belong, rather than in the false positions they occupy in this world. Many who wield worldly power will be humbled and reduced to helplessness. Many who sit in judgement will appear in the dock to be judged. Many who have a high status in life will appear more insignificant than insects. Many who have always had answers for everything in this world will be totally at a loss for words.

When Death Comes

If one closes one's eyes, the whole world appears dark. Everything, from the radiance of the sun and the loftiness of the sky to the verdure of the trees and the splendour of the cities, is plunged into darkness, as if it were not there at all.

The after-life is also an absolute reality which we cannot see, because it belongs to a world in which our vision does not function. At the time of death the veil covering the unseen world will be removed from our eyes and we will be able to gaze on the world of eternity. It will be like having one's eyes closed and then suddenly opening them.

Imagine that a blindfolded person, totally unaware of his predicament, is made to stand in front of a live lion. Suddenly the blindfold is removed. The terror which would be experienced on beholding a lion ready to pounce on him would be far exceeded by the panic which would seize him when suddenly confronted with the world waiting for him after death.

A person who, in the world finds many kinds of support, will suddenly find that there is nothing left to rely on. Friends, a source of constant comfort and pleasure in this world, will have deserted him. His own family, for whom he had been willing to sacrifice anything, will have become alien to him. Material resources, on which he depended entirely, will be of no use. Matters one ignored as trivialities will suddenly loom before one in a form more solid than iron or rock. There will not be a single prop on which one can lean.

The Next World

The present world may seem to lack nothing; but the order of this world has been established with the trial of man in mind. According to God's scheme, only a world which leads up to reward and punishment can be considered ideal and permanent. This is not the case in the present world. So, when the period of trial is over, God will destroy this world and create another more complete one. There the evil will be separated from the righteous, and all will be confronted with the just consequences of their deeds.

The present world is full of strange paradoxes. Here, birds chant hymns of divine praise, while man recites eulogies to himself. Stars and planets continue their voyages without clashing with one another, while man wilfully sets himself on a collision course with others. In this world there is no tree which undermines another, but men spend their lives plotting one another's destruction. Lofty, upright trees show their meekness by casting their shadows on the ground, but if man ascends to any heights he immediately becomes arrogant. This attitude of man's is totally contrary to God's will for His entire creation. Doomsday shall erase these paradoxes, the might of all save God shall be eradicated, and every will save His shall be negated.

When this period of trial has run its course, God will destroy the present world and create another one. There, the righteous and wicked will be separated from one another. The former will reside in paradise and the latter in hell-fire.

As You Sow, So Shall You Reap

Only those who have sown crops can expect a harvest, and what is harvested will be whatever has been sown. The same is true of the next life: there, all men will reap as they have sown. Those who are always jealous, inimical, cruel, and conceited are like those who plant thorn trees. Those who plant thorns will eat thorns in the hereafter. On the other hand, whoever chooses the path of justice, benevolence and acknowledgment of the truth is like the planter of fruit trees. In the next life he will enjoy the sumptuous fruits of his own planting.

People adopt a rebellious stance in this world, yet continue to imagine that they will be raised up amongst God's obedient servants. They are wilfully destructive, but still think that, in eternity, they will have a share in the fruits of constructiveness. Their lives are based on mere words and they believe that these words will take the form of reality in the hereafter. They hear the message of God and refuse to accept it; even so, they have the presumption to think that God will be pleased with them.

God beckons man towards paradise, the abode of eternal comfort and bliss, but man is lost in transitory and illusory pleasures. He does not heed the call of God. He thinks he is gaining while, in fact, he is losing. He believes that the worldly constructions which he is busy erecting will serve him well in the future, but he is only building walls of sand, which will fall never to rise again.

The Inhabitants of Paradise

Paradise is for those, and those alone, who reject all material forms of greatness in order to assert the majesty of Almighty God; who empty their hearts of every other affection and enshrine God therein.

Paradise is for the just, not the cruel, the humble, not the haughty. He who mistreats and degrades others, even when he has grounds for complaint against them forfeits the right to enter Paradise. Plotting to destroy others with whom one is on bad terms and taking delight only in one's own honour and esteem can close the gates of Paradise to one forever. Neither is one fit for Paradise if one's feelings of love and attachment are wounded by criticism of anyone other than God; for Paradise is the domain of those chaste souls who reserve their adoration for God alone, who delight in hearing God's praise and find solace in the sight of God's majesty.

No one who is blind to the truth can enter Paradise, for Paradise is for those alone who associate themselves so closely with the truth that they never fail to see falsehood and reality for what they truly are.

The Straight Path

A train which runs on its tracks will have no trouble in reaching its destination. But should its wheels slip off the rails—no matter to what side—its journey will come to a sudden and disastrous end. Man's journey through life is in some ways on a parallel. If he goes off the rails, it will spell catastrophe. But if he continues to travel along the straight and narrow path which leads directly to God, he will safely reach his destination.

Many examples of human aberration—a 'going-off-the-rails'—can be cited: the satisfying of one's own selfish desires to the exclusion of all else; total absorption in the greatness of some human individual, living or dead; aiming, by preference, at unworthy objectives; obeying impulses of jealousy, hate and vindictiveness, dedicating oneself to any nation or party on the assumption that it is supreme. All of these paths are crooked and diverge from the true way. No one who chooses such a path can ever hope to reach his true goal in life.

It is a sad fact that one tends to stray from the straight path whenever one is obsessed with some thing, person or idea other than God. Whenever one's efforts are directed elsewhere, one is embarking on a detour which can never bring one back to God. Such deviation from the true path can cause man to go totally astray.

The only sure way to spiritual success is to focus one's attentions and efforts on God alone. This is the straight path and involves total attachment to God and a life lived out in complete accordance with His will.

Any path which is not directed towards God is a wrong turning, and will never lead Man to his true destination.

Islam— ## *An Integral Part of Life*

When a stone is dropped into a glass of water, it descends to the bottom and settles to one side. It is in the water but separate from it. On the other hand, if dye is put into the same glass, the dye and water combine. Now the water is not separate from the dye. Both have intermingled in such a way that no one can detect any difference between the two.

The relationship between Islam and a person

should be like that of dye and water, not of stone and water. Islam should not just be an accessory to a Muslim's life: it should merge with his whole being. It should enter into his thoughts, moulding his intellect in its own fashion. Islam should become the eye with which he sees, the tongue with which he speaks, the hands and feet with which he performs his day-to-day functions. Islam should so take possession of a person that it excludes all else. Every statement should bear the stamp of Islam and every action should be dyed in Islamic colours.

If Islam is like a stone in water, then it is not Islam at all. Faith should be absorbed in a person like dye dissolved in water. Just as the emotions of love and hate are felt by the whole body so, when one adopts Islam in the real sense of the world, it should become an issue affecting one's whole existence. The Muslim and Islam should become inseparably attached.

Worship of God

Worship, in form, consists of the performance of certain ritual actions. In essence, it is to form a central focus. From this point of view everyone is worshipping something or the other. It is a rare being who does not cherish some overriding ambition, which he will do his utmost to realize. All men feel some insufficiency in themselves and need some help from outside to make up for it. When one yearns for God alone and puts implicit trust in Him, one is, in reality, worshipping Him. To concentrate one's emotions on something else is to worship others besides Him.

A person who worships God will invoke Him alone, and the prescribed prayers are the day-to-day form which this supplication will take. The worshipper becomes so involved with His Lord that his requirements become minimal; a particular form that this diminution takes is fasting. His adoration of God compels him to strive towards God, and one historic manifestation of his longing is Hajj. He does unto others as he would be done by, and in *zakat*—charity—this takes a regular, practical form.

The whole life of a true worshipper of God, both inwardly and outwardly, becomes an act of worship, bowing only to God and fearing Him alone—putting His considerations first and foremost in all matters. Placing oneself totally in God's hands, one becomes God's own, and God becomes one's own. And one's heart overflows with the love of God.

Forms of Worship

Worship is a reality, not just an outward form. What is true worship? It is an attachment to one object above all else. It presupposes such overwhelming preoccupation with that one object that everything else is reduced to insignificance. Claims to spiritual allegiance are of no value if one's chosen object of worship is other than spiritual.

When one considers a person worthy of being bowed down to, one is actually worshipping that person. When one attaches so much importance to some worldly gain that one tends to overlook all other considerations in order to achieve it, one is actually worshipping that gain. When one associates all one's hopes and ambitions with wealth, one is worshipping wealth.

In like manner, one is worshipping custom when one places it above all other demands. One is worshipping one's own self when, overwhelmed by selfishness and antipathy, one blindly seeks revenge. One is worshipping the standard of living when one is so obsessed with the idea of improving it that one devotes one's entire time and earnings to that end. One is worshipping fame if one is so greedy for rank and prestige that one will do anything to raise one's status in life. One should never forget that man is being tried in this world to determine whether he is willing to devote himself entirely to God to the exclusion of all else, and to give proof of whether he dedicates himself to God, revering Him, depending upon him and serving Him as he should.

A Day in the Life of a Muslim

When a Muslim wakens early in the morning, he thanks God for putting him to sleep and awakening him. After his ablutions, he leaves for the mosque in order to join his brethren in attesting to God's divinity and his own willingness to serve Him. He then ascertains what his Lord expects of him by reading an excerpt from the Qur'an. Then he starts the day's work. There are three prayer times during the day: afternoon, late afternoon and evening. By leaving his work and standing before his Lord at these times, he shows that he gives precedence to God above all else in life.

While satisfying his hunger and thirst, every fibre of his being gives thanks to God. "Lord," he exclaims, "I am wonder-struck at the water you have created for me to quench my thirst with, and the food you have provided for the satisfaction of my hunger!" When success comes his way, he considers it to be a gift from God and offers thanks for it. He considers failure to be the result of his own errors, so he seeks to make amends. When dealing with others, he is conscious of God's presence, which makes him aware of the fact that one day he will be held to account for his actions. When night falls, and he is free of all commitments, he once again washes and, after offering the night prayer, goes to bed. As he drops off to sleep, this prayer is on his lips: Lord, my life and death are in Your hands. Forgive me and have mercy on me." It is evident then that a Muslim does not organize his life-pattern independently. When he arranges his life, it is with God clearly before him.

☙

Giving as God Wills

Man's life and property are gifts of God. He owes everything he possesses to God alone. The only way to give thanks for these innumerable gifts is to dispose of them as God wishes. Such expenditure of one's wealth is symbolic of one's complete trust in God.

Man owes whatever he earns in this world to the fact that God has given him hands and feet to use for this purpose. He has endowed man with eyes and a tongue with which to see and speak. He has blessed him with an intellect which enables him to think and plan. At the same time God has made the world subordinate to man. If the world and that which it contains had not been placed at man's disposal, his physical and mental capabilities alone would never have enabled him to derive any benefit from the world around him. If the wheat grain had not grown in the form of a crop but bad stayed lying on the ground like a pebble, it would have become impossible for man to harvest grain from the land. If the powers of nature had not performed their specific functions, electricity could not have been produced, and vehicles would not have been able to move. Whatever man earns in this world is a direct favour from God. In return, man should spend his earnings in a way which would meet with God's approval. He should use his money to help the poor and spend of the wealth which God has granted him in the ways of God has specified.

Real charity is that which is given for God's sake alone, not for fame, self-esteem or worldly reward. Wealth saves one from worldly hardship; that which is given away for God's sake saves one from the hardships of the life after death.

Islamic Character

An Islamic character is a divine character. It is to treat others with the same generosity and charity as God shows to man. The Quran has set the pattern in this matter by stating: "If you are merciful, forgiving and magnanimous, then God is the Forgiving, the Merciful." That is to say that if a relationship with someone turns sour, or some difference of opinion occurs, one should adopt a posture similar to God's. He forgives people their mistakes and does not deprive them of His mercies because of their errors; one should act in like manner. If something is said which hurts one's feelings, or one is treated in a disconcerting manner, the transgressor should not be turned against for this reason alone; rather one should overlook his mistakes and treat him as if nothing had happened.

To put it in a word, magnanimity is what marks an Islamic character. Generally one treats others according to what they have said or done with regard to one. A Muslim should transcend such considerations in his treatment of others. His reactions should be moulded by God's commandments, which means maintaining the highest standard of helpfulness and benevolence towards others. If one cannot actually be of use to others, then one must at least avoid harming them, and must spare them any suffering on account of ill-judged words and actions. Islamic character ceases to be such on any plane lower than this.

Humility—
The Foundation of Unity

The basis of unity is humility. If everyone puts others before himself, then the question of friction does not arise, for disunity stems from everyone putting himself first and wishing that he and his utterances should be given supremacy, no matter what the circumstances. If no one considered himself superior, what would there be to quarrel about?

Clashes of interest and outlook are bound to occur in a society where people live in close contact with each other. When this happens, superiority complexes are apt to surface. Everybody tends to feel sure that his own opinion is correct, that his rights supersede others', and that his own interest must be protected at all costs. Considerations such as these alienate people from one another, which results in disharmony, and if all parties remain adamant, friction can do little but escalate. If, however, one of the parties to a dispute adopts a humble attitude and is willing to stand down, then discord will vanish automatically, and harmony will prevail. Unity can exist only by sinking personal differences, by recognizing the rights of others to disagree and, where agreement is impossible, by bringing matters to a conclusion by agreeing to disagree in a spirit of goodwill.

It is only natural in a society that opinions should clash and grievances arise. These things cannot be eliminated entirely. There will be unity only when people cease to harbour grievances, and when they can live in harmony notwithstanding their differences.

Who Should Preach?

A sage once said that the desire to preach should have the same compulsive quality about it as the desire to satisfy any other normal human urge. Preaching is not like playing a record; nor should it be aimed at eliciting applause from an appreciative audience. Preaching is an externalisation of inner conviction. It is communication to others of a discovered reality; to be a living witness to a truth long hidden from people's eyes. This does not mean just putting a few words together; it is an extremely difficult task. One can only accomplish this task when one feels so desperate an urge to convey one's message that one is ready in the process to face unpopularity and self-sacrifice.

The same applies to writing. Before putting pen to paper, one should study so much that knowledge of itself starts overflowing from one's mind. It is only after sifting through all the available material on any relevant topic, and feeling an irresistible urge to add something of one's own, that one should begin to write. Those who write without experience or inspiration are only defacing the paper on which they write, and those who speak without feeling the compulsion to do so are only adding to noise pollution.

Preaching is not a game: it is representation of God on earth; it is only those who have effaced themselves before God who qualify for this privilege. Those who try to preach without such qualifications do greater harm than good.

Acknowledgment of the Truth

God manifests Himself on earth through truth. Disbelief in the truth is disbelief in God. One can perpetrate no greater crime on earth than to refuse to accept the truth after it has been made plain. Truth emanates from God, so whoever rejects it is, in fact, rejecting God.

There is nothing strange about the truth. It is inherent in human nature. Since it is so familiar to' mankind, why do people fail to accept it? The answer is that they are psychologically inhibited from doing so.

Acceptance of the truth might disrupt their materially-oriented life-pattern. They might have to prepare themselves for a lowering of their worldly status. If the truth is taught by some insignificant person against whom they are prejudiced, they feel reluctant to acknowledge the veracity of his message. Psychological impediments such as these dominate the mind and prevent straight thinking. They cause one to reject something which a little honest thought would surely have led one to accept as the truth.

Since man is being tested in this world, God does not make himself manifest in visible form; He appears in the form of truth. Man must endeavour to recognize truth as enshrining God and bow down before it. Whenever truth appears on earth, it is as if God has appeared in all His majesty. If one rejects it on the grounds of prejudice, pride or expediency, then one has rejected God Himself. This action shows that one has failed to recognize God in the truth. One has put oneself above God and given precedence to one's own requirements. God will have scant regard for such people on the Day of Judgement and, on that day, whomsoever God scorns will find no refuge on earth or in heaven. They will wander helplessly, forever abject and forlorn.

Three Types of Human Being

On the highest plan of Islamic faith, one should fear God, always turning to Him, and acting as if one knows that He is watching over one. People who are so inclined may never have seen God, but they live more in awe of Him than of all the visible powers. When they reach God their hearts will already have been turned towards Him, and God desires and loves such servants. When they enter the life of eternity, having borne worldly affliction for God's sake, their Lord will felicitate them, and bid them come inside a paradise of fresh green gardens, in which they shall forever abide. "There", as the Qur'an states, "their desires will be more than fulfilled by God!" (50:31-35).

Then there are those who believe in God and do good. They may sometimes err, but they never persist in their misconduct. They acknowledge their faults and constantly seek God's forgiveness. They repent and incessantly attempt to make amends to their Lord. Hopefully, God will be merciful to them. When they turn towards God, God also relents towards them, for He is the All-Forgiving, the All-Merciful (9:102).

There are yet others who have taken to self-worship, materialism and arrogance. They never, for

God's sake, constrain themselves in thought, word or deed. They live for themselves rather than for God, and think of the world rather than the after-life. How, then, can they hope to find a place of honour in the everlasting world of God? Nothing but hell-fire awaits such people in eternity. (11:15-16).

The Reward of God

Closeness to God should mean that He is ever in one's thoughts. Awareness of God's greatness should reduce one's own being to insignificance. Heaven and hell should be so much a part of faith, that one should be more concerned with well-being (or affliction) in the after-life than one's condition in the present world. On so high a spiritual plain should one be that one's faults should begin to appear in the same light as an enemy's. Personal prejudice should play no part in decision-making and even those with whom one disagrees, or against whom one bears some grudge, should be prayed for from the heart. Denial of truth should be seen as self-destruction and destroying another's home should be regarded as tantamount to setting one's own home ablaze. Such is the God-fearing life and only those who lead it will be given a place in God's paradise.

To His true servants in this world, God has

promised supremacy. But this is not the real reward for their piety; it is merely a forerunner of the true recompense which will await them in eternity. It is then that they will be honoured with everlasting supremacy. God will rid them of their fear and grief, and accord to them His everlasting beneficence.

The Islamic Life

Islam can be summed up very briefly: fear of God and benevolence towards others. A Muslim is one who realizes God's omnipotence and man's utter helplessness in comparison. The power which man apparently wields has been given to him only so that he may be tested by it. When his trials are at an end, God will reveal to him a hitherto unseen world. Then, astoundingly, God's divinity on the one hand and man's total helplessness on the other, will become as plain as daylight. There will be such revelations of reality on that day as man will have no choice but to accept.

The Muslim is fully able to anticipate the advent of this day before its actual arrival. He lives as if he is actually seeing God watching over him. When he speaks, his faith holds his tongue in check, constraining him to speak the truth or else remain silent. When he walks, it is as if God were in front of him, forcing him to proceed and he would never dare incur his Lord's displeasure.

Such a person bears nothing but goodwill towards God's servants. He regards them with compassion, for that is the way God looks upon them. When he has dealings with others, he judges himself by the same just criteria and values as the Creator and Master of the universe will eventually apply to all beings.

Life in Accordance with Reality

What is Islam? Islam means living in accordance with nature; living as one ought, face to face with reality. Man did not create himself: he was created by God. To live in accordance with reality, then, is to acknowledge the greatness of God and show appreciation of His favours. The emotions of love and fear are inherent in man. He wants something on which he can depend and upon which he can focus his efforts. If he lives in accordance with reality, he will focus all his attention on God alone for, besides Him, all things have been created: nothing besides Him has any power.

Adam is the father of all past, present and future men, so life in accordance with reality is one of benevolence to others, as if one were dealing with one's own brothers and sisters. Everyone has a conscience, which favours justice and despises cruelty and injustice. Life in accordance with reality, then, is one of kindness and justness. Death is bound to come one day. It will deprive everyone of his worldly possessions, so one who lives in accordance with reality will look at the ups and downs of life as transitory and trivial. Everybody, irrespective of worldly status, should be regarded as God's servant. When one is confronted with a truth one might feel disposed to deny it. But one should realize that, one day, everyone will have to accept truth and falsehood for what they are. One should willingly accept today what one will have to accept tomorrow.

From God's Point of View

If one wears ordinary spectacles, everything will appear as it is. If, on the other hand, one wears dark glasses, everything will take on different hue, depending on the colour of the glasses. The same applies to the human intellect. When one observes someone, one does so through the lenses of one's own intellect. If the lens is clear, then everything will appear as it is. If it is tinted, then everything, regardless of its true nature, will take on a false appearance.

The human mind is either God-oriented or self-oriented. It sees people through either divine or personal lenses. These are two very different ways of seeing things. Those who look at matters from God's point of view are realistic in their outlook. They judge things on merit, not on the basis of their own biased opinions. They see people as they really are, for that is how God views them. Others see things quite differently. They view people in the light of their own interests and prejudices. Their friends are beautiful, their enemies are ugly. Members of their own clique are "white", strangers "black". The true Muslim sees everybody from God's point of view. He does not judge others on the basis of personal opinion.

It is this divine vision which really makes a person. It makes one treat others as they should be treated. It makes one realistic as far as this world is concerned and righteous with regard to the world hereafter.

Care in All Matters

An unbeliever tends to be insensitive, but a believer should have a heightened awareness of what is right and wrong. The believer's sensitivity is not limited to God and objects generally regarded as sacrosanct; it embraces every object of creation.

When dealing with others, be they weak or strong,

a believer is always scrupulous about giving them their full due as prescribed by God. He always treats animals humanely. If he is forced to exterminate some pest, he does not do so in a cruel manner. His sensitive nature would not allow him to cut down a tree or crush a flower for no good reason. He is careful not to be extravagant in his use of water, for that would amount to misuse of a gift of God.

Once a person has had the circumspection and sensitivity of faith instilled in him his disposition and actions are moulded accordingly. Faith controls his manners, speech, movements, dealings, and utilization of animate and inanimate objects. Even in emotional situations, he does not act rashly; he does not treat anybody cruelly or unsympathetically.

True belief involves a scrupulous awareness of the fact that God is watching over one, and will take one to task for what one does, both in secret and in public. A man thoroughly imbued with faith will necessarily be a more caring person.

Relinquishing Power for God

All power in this world belongs to God. None else has any strength. Nevertheless, God has granted man freedom in this world so that he may be tested.

Man is the only creature free to exercise his will in a world which is otherwise entirely subjugated to the will of God. God wants to see how man utilizes the power and free will with which he has been endowed. If he is realistic, he will submit to God. Otherwise, deluded by his apparent freedom, he will continue in his rebellious ways.

Paradise is for those who have power, but disclaim all pretence to it; who fear God, though they are in a position to do the opposite; who have the chance to attach importance to themselves, but refrain from doing so, putting God first.

Such people consider that they are directly provided for by God, though such provision is concealed beneath a veil of worldly causes. They have opportunities to oppress and exploit people, but fear of God prevents them from doing so. At times they feel tempted to indulge in anger, hate and revenge, but patience cools their anger, and forgiveness obliterates any hostility or vengeance which stirs in their hearts. Where people are full of praise for them, they are balanced enough to retain their humility. God may have endowed them with abundant wealth, but they spend their wealth as God would wish. It is not personal satisfaction that they seek; their only desire is to please their Lord. They do not live for themselves; they live only for God.

The exquisite world of paradise is for those who, of their own free will, subordinate themselves to the will of God. It is reserved for those who adhere to God's path, though they have been given rein enough to stray from it if they so desire. It will be the reward of those who, though not compelled to do so, obey God's commandments.

The Trial of Man

Life is one long trial. The great paradox is that while some enjoy life, others undergo continuous suffering. In reality, however, all are the same, for their actions are being scrutinized. Everyone is being examined; it is only the conditions under which this examination is being conducted that vary.

Another factor in the trial of man is that God has made some weak and others strong. There is always the temptation to succumb to the mighty and to exploit the weak. But to do this is to take the surest road to hell. Only those who consider what is right, irrespective of circumstances or of the individuals they deal with, will prove themselves worthy of paradise, for it is often the underdog who is in the right and the mighty who are in the wrong. Even when others behave in a troublesome way, the best way to react is with mildness and circumspection, and no matter what the provocation, one should endeavour to be impartial and just.

The manner in which people respond to the various situations which confront them in life will determine their eternal abode. Those who yield to the mighty and oppress the weak will surely be punished in hell, and they would do well to remember that there are two paths which open out before them every day, one of which leads to hell and the other to paradise.

Testing
Man's Fitness

Man has complete freedom of will in this world, but only God can actually make things happen. Man is just being put to the test on earth. His reactions to various circumstances are being scrutinized.

Some respond to events in a patient, just and reasonable manner. Their actions earn them credit. Others react quite differently. Their hot-headedness, cruelty, and blindness to the truth earn them nothing but blame. Some profess to be Muslims. But if they adopt a disparaging, deceptive and malicious attitude towards others, their claim is immediately proved false. God will particularly help those whom they wrong in order to show where the truth lies. Some uphold the truth, yet they are left in a helpless and forlorn state. Others are blind to the truth, yet have every conceivable worldly luxury at their disposal. This situation may seem paradoxical, but it occurs for a reason: to set apart those who cling to externals and deserve to be classed along with other deniers of the truth.

Everything man experiences in this world, be it power or weakness, wealth or poverty, is a test. Worldly triumph is no cause to rejoice; nor should worldly loss cause one grief. Both winner and loser are being tested to see how they react to their respective situations. It is on the basis of this reaction that they will be adjudged fit for either heaven or hell.

Some Earn the World, Others Eternity

A man set on making money, chooses a lucrative profession and devotes all his time and energies to it. If his efforts yield financial reward, well and good. If not, he is upset about his choice of profession. If he is after fame and prestige, he looks for a career which holds the promise of publicity. He thrives on popularity and esteem. If these things elude him, he feels as if all is lost. If a man is thirsty for power, his overriding ambition is to rule others. He longs to have people under him and to control their fortunes. Such people seek worldly reward for their actions, but no matter how much they manage to acquire in this world, they will have no share in the hereafter.

God's true servant on the other hand, seeks everlasting reward for his actions and concentrates on an eternal goal. While people are busy in worldly affairs, he functions in the silent world of nature. While people display their fervour in public, he struggles on in seclusion. He has no thought of worldly fame or success. He longs solely for God's mercy and grace. Outwardly he belongs to this world, but mentally and emotionally he dwells in the next. People are absorbed in the world of forms, whereas he is lost in God's hidden cosmos.

Stimulus and Response

Human character can be guarded from the way people respond to day-to-day events. Everything that happens affects one in one way or another. The kind of response we make to what is going on around us is determined by our mentality. If one is unmindful of God, one will react in whatever manner one's own desires and interests demand. If, however, one's faith is strong, each and every event throughout one's entire life reminds one of God; the entire range of one's emotions is then concentrated not on oneself, but on God.

Fortunes in life never cease to fluctuate. Ease is soon followed by hardship. It is never long before praise and approval give way to criticism and accusation. No sooner do events begin to follow a satisfactory course than they suddenly take a turn for the worse. Ups and downs of this nature are all in the nature of a trial. If one is to succeed in life's trial, these changes of fortune should turn one more and more towards God and away from the self, and, humble and resigned when stricken by misfortune, one should be thankful in one's heart for the happiness and comfort granted by God.

People's response to various circumstances is being put to the test on earth. This is what their worldly trial really consists of. If given wealth and power, they become proud, then they are failures, but if they remain humble under the same circumstances, they have succeeded. They have failed if they are obstinate and contemptuous towards their rivals or opponents: if they are unjust to others, they are bound to come to grief themselves: if they are fair to all and sundry, they will emerge triumphant from life's trial.

It's Selection Time

The constellation closest to earth contains at least two hundred million stars and countless such constellations are scattered throughout space. The universe is incredibly vast but, as far as we know, there is only one solar system and, within that solar system, our planet, earth, is situated. There is no planet to compare with earth in the entire universe and, upon it, dwells that unique being called man. Man lives. He moves and talks. He sees and hears. He thinks and understands. He is responsible for his actions. There is no doubt about man's uniqueness. But the question remains: why has God created him so? The answer is: in order to select those who will abide in the even more exquisite and ideal world of paradise.

The world is full of creatures who, subject to God, involuntarily do as God bids them. God wills it, however, that man should be obedient of his own accord. God seeks those who are willing to renounce the power that they possess; who manage to see God despite His invisibility; who belong to the hereafter, though they dwell on earth; who accept and obey, though they are capable of denial and rebellion. Those who display such propensities in the world will be welcomed to paradise in the hereafter. Paradise is an ideal abode for ideal individuals. So enchanting and alluring will it be, that no one in it will ever have a feeling of tedium. No pain or apprehension will mar its delight. Man will find there all that he desires.

❦

People of God

Everyone lives for something or another. Some live for their families. Some for money. Some for worldly tribute and power. A life which revolves around these things cannot be a life of faith. A life of faith is one lived for God's sake alone. When one lives for God, one's entire life revolves around Him. One's thoughts and desires are focused on Him alone. One thinks about what pleases and displeases God when one speaks. One limits one's movements to the bounds that God has laid down.

The human brain inevitably forms some sort of response to any message that it receives. Those who live for God will produce divinely inspired responses. Their utterances will not be based on the promptings of their own selves. They consider what will be acceptable to God and what will be cast aside when they come before Him. If their conscience tells them that certain words are displeasing to God, then they avoid them. They only say what they know God would like them to.

When one faces some problem, one immediately

chooses a method of dealing with it. If one lives in God, then one will not act on impulse; one will consider what is just and unjust in God's sight. Though fame and wealth may lie on the path of injustice, one forsakes that path. One adheres to the path of justice, though it may incur worldly loss and unpopularity. One looks at everything from God's point of view, and not from any other standpoint.

Abstaining
From Baseness

A believer makes mistakes, but does not stoop to baseness. Mistakes are often made in sudden fits of emotion, but, when the passion cools, one becomes conscious of the error and feels ashamed of one's own wrongdoing. The next step is to seek out the wronged person, beg forgiveness and make amends. If compensation can be given, well and good. If not, one prays: "Lord, forgive my mistake and accept this salutary prayer from me on behalf of the person I have wronged!"

A mean person would behave in quite a different way, for meanness is a permanent state of mind rather than a temporary condition. A person who has stooped so low feels neither shame nor any urge to make amends for what has passed. In fact, he would be happy to see his opponent suffer more. If he has a grievance against someone, he is not satisfied merely with a severance of relations, but does his utmost to lay that person low. He makes slanderous accusations and concocts vicious plots against him. He does not just point out a person's errors; he seeks to discredit that person completely and isolate him from the rest of society. He tries to undo whatever his enemy has accomplished and bring all his gain to nought. This all shows a lack of magnanimity and, as such, is unbecoming to a believer.

Refusal to admit one's faults is contemptible. It is likewise despicable to favour one's own kith and kin, while treating others with disdain. A base person cannot rise above envy and vindictiveness. Such a person is a long way from God and close to the devil.

A Believer Lives for God

Asmall infant owes everything to his parents. His life revolves around them. So a believer's life should revolve around God. God should dwell in his reflections. He should fear and love God alone. He should do everything for God's sake. He should put total trust in God, his Guardian and Protector.

Usually, people live for mundane things. That is why they never find contentment. They either live for personalities or for worldly splendours. Either their families mean everything to them, or else they have made prestige and wealth their ultimate goals in life. Some are obsessed with hatred. Some live to thwart, humiliate or ruin others. All these ways of living are based on false notions. They are placing total reliance on things which are ephemeral and out of place in God's cosmic order. These things can never give man true peace of mind. They do not allow one to proceed along the divine path, which is the only road to salvation. In this world all things live for God. If man succours himself otherwise, he will eventually find himself helpless and on a false path.

A startling transformation takes place in a person who starts living for God. He finds silence more gratifying than speech. He is happier to obey than to rebel, to forgive than to hold grudges, he tries to hide other's faults. He is unassuming and self-effacing. He is not interested in occupying a privileged position.

Setting Oneself Right

A traveller buys a ticket for a certain destination, then boards a train bound for another. He does not realize his error until the train has left the station. Imagine how he feels! The seat in which he was relaxing now gives him nothing but discomfort. As soon as the train reaches the next station, he will get off in order to return and catch the next train.

A believer's attitude to his eternal journey is the same as this traveller's. Whenever anything happens which will divert him from the path to his eternal destination and will adversely affect him in the next life, he is extremely ashamed of himself. He wastes no time in admitting his mistake. He gets his bearings and immediately starts travelling in the right direction.

The true believer may err, but he turns away from his wrongdoing. He may be angry for some reason, but then his anger cools and he becomes forgiving. Self-respect does not prevent him from admitting his mistakes. If, however, a person persists in his evil ways; if he is not ready to forgive others on being offended by them; if he refuses to admit his own mistakes and shortcomings; then, though he may lay claim to being a true Muslim, he is not one in God's sight. If a person does not want to admit his faults in this world, he will have no difficulty in finding words to justify them. In some cases worldly status is enough to screen a person's faults. In eternity, however, such things will be of no help to anybody. There, realities will become so plain that even the blind will be able to see them.

Thinking on a Higher Plane

In stormy weather small, weak-winged birds are trapped by the storm. Large birds, with their strong wings, can fly above it. A person who can ride above his circumstances is like one of these big birds which can ride any storm.

Likewise there are two levels of thinking. Some think in relation to their immediate circumstances. Their thoughts are inextricably linked to the issues in which they are involved. Others, like big birds of the storm, rise above their immediate situation. Their thoughts are not affected by circumstances. They form their opinions on a higher level.

Believers think in 'big bird' style. They rise above their circumstances. Even when in trouble, they are thankful to God. In the most distraught of conditions they stick to their religion. They are benevolent and just towards others, even if they have grievances against them. Their personalities develop irrespective of circumstances. They are not products of situations, dwelling as they do outside life's storm, and not allowing themselves to be tossed about in its turbulent winds.

Unbelievers react to life's problems in an unreflective way, whereas believers always look at matters positively. Unbelievers increase their own worth at the expense of others; believers know that the only way to true success lies in developing one's own potential. Unbelievers are concerned with worldly things; believers with eternity. An unbelieving heart is attached to human beings; a heart full of faith is always with God.

Realizing One's Own Mistakes

People who are in the habit of filling out their sentences with unnecessary words are usually quite unaware of their own habit. If however, someone else, does the same thing, they notice it immediately.

This is a common human fault. People are usually well-informed about others' faults. They ferret out shortcomings in other people, but pretend to know nothing about what they and their friends do wrong.

Yet, it is acknowledgement of one's own faults rather than skill in noticing those of others which will benefit one in God's presence. To notice others' mistakes is to show God that one has been altogether too attentive to worldly matters. On the Day of Judgement, a severe punishment awaits one who has been guilty of their error.

God has given man the power of distinguishing between good and evil. People should use this power to avoid paths leading to hell and keep to the road destined for paradise. If one is following a false path oneself, one's exhortation of others to the true way shows an obvious misuse of one's discretion. One is using it to accelerate one's own journey to hell, for, to preach what one fails to practice is an offence in the eyes of God; it is not an action which will earn one any credit.

$$\clubsuit$$

A Believer's Wealth

It is written in the Qur'an; "To those who hoard up gold and silver and do not spend it in the way of God, give tidings of a painful doom. The day will surely come when their treasures will be heated in the fire of hell, and their foreheads and their flanks and their backs will be branded therewith. They will be told:

"Here are the riches which you hoarded for yourselves. Now taste what you used to hoard" (9:35). When this verse was revealed, the companions of the Prophet wondered what kind of wealth they should accumulate instead. Umer, may God be pleased with him, went to the Prophet and put this question to him on their behalf. The Prophet, may God's peace and blessings be upon him, replied: "Each of you should acquire a heart grateful to God, and a tongue accustomed to His remembrance, and a believing spouse who will be of assistance in matters relating to eternity." (Ibn Majah)

Wealth is of use only when it can solve the problems of life. The greatest problem of believers concerns the next world, so they consider real wealth to be that which will be of use to them there. In order to obtain such wealth, one should always be thankful to God for His blessings. One's attachment to God should be such that He is always in one's mind and heart. If one has set one's sights on life everlasting, one will prefer one's companion in life to be similarly disposed. There is no greater wealth in life than a partner who, instead of enticing one towards ephemeral, mundane pleasures, assists one on the path of eternity.

People see wealth in gold and silver, but a believer's wealth is God. That which brings him nearer to his Lord and makes him eligible for God's blessings in the life to come, is to him of supreme importance.

Making a Living

A believer should look at his means of subsistence as a necessity; he should never make these means his goal in life. His objective should be eternity, and worldly things should be just the bare necessities. The difference between believers' and unbelievers' attitudes to the world is essentially one of priorities. Unbelievers aim to make as much money as possible: believers should aim to make a living as honestly as they can. Unbelievers expect their careers to pave the way to the fulfillment of their ambitions: believers should merely seek to be independent of others. Unbelievers live on a mundane plane—they want to receive their earnings in this world. Believers live on an other-worldly plane and wish to see their efforts rewarded in eternity. They are just filling in time in this world. Their ambitions will be fulfilled in the next.

Making a living is a matter of crucial importance to every individual. No one is exempt from the struggle for subsistence. Islam simply makes sure that it remains a matter of necessity and does not become the sole objective of anyone's life. The Islamic view is that one's livelihood should not become the be-all and end-all of a person's life; that one's heart should be with God, even when engaged in one's worldly tasks; that one should have total trust in God.

Unbelievers use wealth to improve their standard of living. Believers, on the other hand, spend it on themselves only in so far as is necessary; the remainder they give away in God's path. Unbelievers consider money as a means of future security, but believers use it to ensure their prosperity in life-everlasting. Making a living is important for everyone, but believers should ensure that this task is accomplished in an honest manner, and then be happy with their lot. Unbelievers tend to be arbitrary in their methods and never cease to want more.

Education

K nowledge is of two kinds: that which has been set forth in the Qur'an and the Hadith, and that which we acquire by our own research and endeavours. The first form of knowledge acquaints us with our Lord. It explains the issues we will have to face in the everlasting world that is waiting for us after death. It shows us how preparation can be made in this life to meet those issues. The second form of knowledge provides solutions to the everyday, social and economic problems we encounter in this world.

Muslims should seek both forms of knowledge.

They should be familiar with both secular and religious sciences, although they vary in the degree of their importance. Knowledge of the Qur'an and Hadith should be the basic aim in life, and knowledge of other sciences a worldly necessity. Without knowledge of the Qur'an and the Hadith, one cannot understand what must be done in this world for one to earn everlasting salvation. The secular sciences, on the other hand, guide us in worldly matters. They instruct us in the practicalities of life. Knowledge of the Qur'an and the Hadith shows the way to building for eternity; other knowledge is a guide to worldly development alone.

It is just as important for a Muslim to study various branches of knowledge as it is for anyone else, but the Muslim should differentiate between aim and necessity. He studies the Qur'an and the Hadith for different reasons from those which prompt him to seek worldly knowledge.

The Mosque

Whereas there is a plethora of old forts in most countries, they are remarkably scarce in Muslim lands. The skyline of Muslim towns is dominated more by the lofty minarets of mosques. This shows the difference between the Islamic and non-Islamic temperament. Non-Muslims rely on their own strategies; Muslims place total trust in God. This explains why non-Muslims have always erected forts for their own protection and security, while Muslims have built mosques wherever they achieved supremacy. Massive castles testify to man's greatness, whereas mosques, in which Muslims glorify God, are a reminder to present and future generations of the greatness of God.

A mosque is, locally, a focal point for Muslims, just as the Ka'bah in Mecca is for Muslims all over the world. The Ka'bah is a world religious centre and the mosque a local one. That is why the same word for the direction in which one faces to pray—*qiblah* has been used in the Qur'an for both the Holy Ka'bah and also local mosques. Prayer is a symbol of a life of faith, and houses of worship, mosques, are for the performance of that act of faith on a local level and, in the case of Mecca and Medina, on an international level.

Muslims gather five times a day to pray in the mosque. The mosque is their natural religious centre. That is why the Prophet encouraged us to build mosques in the centres of towns. The situation of mosques, and the activities which are conducted in them, are in themselves an invitation to people to come together for worship of their Lord.

Islam and Infidelity

Islam is acknowledgement and infidelity is denial. Man may seem to be free to do or say what he likes in the world, but, in reality, everything belongs to God. Whatever anybody has is His gift. Nobody, save God, has any power. God is always in a position to seize and punish man. Islam is acknowledgement of this fact and believers live in accordance with it. Infidelity is denial and unwillingness to base one's life on a realistic foundation.

A man can put his hand into a blazing fire if he wants to, but he refrains from doing so: he bows to reality. The freedom which man seems to enjoy in this world is only a test. Only if man is free, can it become clear who chooses to rebel against reality and who acknowledges it and submits to God. If one accepts God's divinity and bases one's life on reality, then one has truly embraced Islam and can enjoy God's everlasting blessings. If one denies this reality and refuses to accept God as Master, and be His servant, then one's action amounts to unbelief and one will be exposed to dreadful punishment on the Day of Judgement.

To accept the Islamic way entails undergoing an immense change within oneself. It means that one's thoughts, actions and treatment of others take on the most proper and most exemplary form imaginable, for one's whole life will then be in harmony with reality. Unbelievers tend to contradict reality in everything that they do. Their actions can only lead them to their doom.

The Relationship Between Man and God

It is written in the Qur'an: "And when My servants question you concerning Me, tell them that I am close at hand. I answer the prayer of the suppliant when he cries to Me. So let them hear My call and let them trust in Me, in order they may be led aright." (2:186). This shows that the relationship between man and God is reciprocal: man offers God what he has, then God bestows His favours in return. Man offers his Lord a gift of realization, piety and thankfulness. In return, God provides him with eternal guidance and prosperity.

Man can deal with any problem in either of two ways: the pious and morally proper way, or the way in which such values are abandoned. The correct answer to the call of God is for one to use one's intellect to ascertain the right course of action and then follow it, difficult as it may seem. One then automatically avoids the easy, though misguided, way.

Sometimes one is faced with the choice between callous and unjust action on the one hand and righteous, fair treatment on the other. If one answers God's call as it should be answered, one will not flinch from the righteous path and will refrain from oppression and cruelty.

Man is free to consider what he has, within him and outside, to be the result of chance; alternatively he may look at it all as the fruits of his efforts; or he can acknowledge reality and consider it all as having come from God. A person who adopts this latter course will answer the call of God implicit in every blessing by exclaiming, "Lord, You are the bestower and You have given us everything!" When one has offered one's mind and heart to God in this way, then God will provide one with guidance, which means a righteous life in this world and eternal paradise in the next.

❦

Do As You Would be Done By

Why is it that supplications made to God often go unheeded? The reason is that people ask God for that which they themselves are not prepared to give to others. They ask God for protection against oppression, but they are the first to inflict it on others when they have the chance. They ask God to safeguard their lives and property, yet are quick to kill and seize someone else's property if they can. They ask God for an honourable life, yet are quite happy to humiliate others. They ask God to protect them from enemy plots, yet they plot the destruction of anybody with whom they disagree. One must be sincere in whatever one is praying for. One's supplication should emanate from one's innermost being. It should not just be empty words. When one is sincere, one's life becomes devoid of contradictions. No difference remains between what one prays for and what one practices. If one really detests cruelty and objects to others indulging in it, then one will never resort to it oneself. If one stoops to persecuting others, then one cannot be sincere when one protests about being persecuted. The prayer of a person who does not put words into action will not be graced by divine acceptance. If one is causing conflict among people, yet at the same time praying for harmony, one's prayer must seem more like a jest to God, and can earn one only retribution. For prayers to be acceptable, it is essential that one should give others what one seeks for oneself. One should treat others with the same mercy and compassion as one desires for oneself. Otherwise one's prayer will be an offence rather than a supplication before God.

PART THREE

The Good Life

God is One

Say: God is One, The Eternal God. He begot none, nor was He begotten. None is equal to Him (112:1-4).

Mankind, worship your Lord, who has created you and those before you, so that you may ward off evil; who has made the earth a couch for you and the sky a canopy; and has sent down water from the sky, thereby producing fruits for you to eat. So do not knowingly set up rivals to God (2:21-22).

God does not forgive partners being ascribed to Him. He forgives whom He will all other sins. Whoever ascribes partners to God has strayed far from the truth (4:116).

God—The Sublime, the Tremendous

Allah—there is no God save Him, the Ever-living, the Eternal. Neither drowsiness nor sleep overtakes Him. To Him belongs all that is in the heavens and on the earth. Who can intercede with Him save by His leave? He knows what lies before humans and what is after them, and they encompass nothing of His knowledge save what He wills. His throne comprises both the heavens and the earth, and He is never weary of preserving them. He is the Sublime the Tremendous (2:255).

God's Signs

Your Lord is God, who created the skies and the earth in six periods, then ascended His Throne. He throws the veil of night over day. Swiftly they follow one another. The sun, moon and stars are subservient to His command. His is the creation, His is the command. Blessed be God, the Lord of the worlds. Call on your Lord humbly and secretly; He does not love the transgressors. Do not bring corruption to the land after things have been set right. Pray to Him fearfully, eagerly. God's mercy is within reach of the righteous. He sends forth the winds as harbingers of His mercy till, when they bear a heavy cloud, We drive it to a dead land and cause rain to descend thereon, bringing forth all manner of fruit. Thus We will raise the dead to life; perchance you will take heed. And as for the good land, its vegetation comes forth by the leave of its Lord. But poor and scant are the fruits which spring from barren soil. Thus We make plain Our signs for those who render thanks (7:54-58).

In Heaven
and on Earth

So glory be to God morning and evening. Praise be to Him in the heavens and on earth, at twilight and at noon. He brings forth the living from the dead, and the dead from the living, and He revives the earth after it is dead. Likewise you shall be raised to life. And by one of His signs He created you from dust; now behold you are human beings, ranging widely. And by another of His signs He created for you, of yourselves, spouses that you might find repose in them and has planted love and kindness in your hearts. Surely there are signs in this for people who reflect. Among His other signs are the creation of the heavens and the earth and the variety of your tongues and hues. Surely there are signs in this for those who know. And by another of His signs is your slumbering by night and your seeking of His bounty by day. Surely in that are signs for those who hear. The lightning which He shows you to inspire fear and hope is yet another of His signs. He sends down water from the sky, thereby reviving the earth after it is dead. Surely in this there are signs for a people who understand. The heavens and the earth are firm by His command; then when He calls you, suddenly, from the earth you shall emerge. To Him belongs everything in the heavens and on earth; all are obedient to Him. He it is who originates creation, then reproduces it, and it is easier for Him. His is the loftiest attribute in heaven and on earth. He is the Mighty, the Wise One. (30:17-27).

The Cosmic Call

It is God who splits the grain and the date stone. He brings forth the living from the dead, and the dead from the living. Such is God. How then can you turn away from Him? He splits the sky into dawn. He has made the night for repose and the sun and the moon for reckoning. Such is the ordinance of God, the Mighty, the Wise. It is He who has created for you the stars, so that you may be guided by them in the darkness by land and sea. We have made plain our signs for people who understand. It is He who sent down water from the sky. With it We bring forth the shoot of every plant and then We have brought forth its green leaf and from it close-compounded grain; and out of the date-palm, from its pollen, dates thick-clustered, ready to the hand; and gardens of grapes, olives and pomegranates, like and unlike one another. Look upon their fruits when they fructify and ripen. Surely in all this are signs for people who believe. Yet they ascribe as partners to Him the jinn, though He created them, and they impute to Him sons and daughters without any knowledge. Glory be to Him and exalted be He above what they describe. He is the Creator of the heavens and the earth. How can He have a son, when there is for Him no consort; when He created all things and He has knowledge of all things? (6:96-104).

❧

Lord of the Great Throne

Did you think that We created you in vain and that you would never be returned to Us? Exalted be God, the true King. There is no God but He, the Lord of the great throne. And whoever invokes any other deity besides God—a deity of whose divinity he has no proof—with his Lord alone will be his reckoning. The unbelievers shall never prosper. And say: Lord, forgive and have mercy, for You are the best of those that show mercy (23:115-118).

Love for God

In the creation of the heavens and the earth; in the alternation of night and day; in the ships that sail the ocean with cargoes beneficial to men; in the water which God sends down from the sky and with which He revives the dead earth after its death, dispersing over it all kinds of beasts; in the swirling of the winds and in the clouds that are driven between earth and sky; surely in this there are signs for people who understand. Yet there are some people who choose from other beings besides God, as rivals to God, loving them as God alone should be loved—whereas those who believe love God more than all else. If the evildoers could only see, when they behold the doom, that power lies with God alone and that God is severe in punishment. When those who were followed disown their followers and they behold the doom, and their cords are cut asunder, those who followed will say, "If only a return were possible for us, we would disown them, as they have disowned us." Thus God will show them their own work as anguish for them. They shall never emerge from the Fire. Mankind, eat of what is in the earth lawful and wholesome, and do not follow in the steps of Satan, for he is your sworn enemy. He commands you only to evil and indecency and that you should assert about God what you do not know (2:164-169).

God's Prophets

Those who believe and have not tainted their belief with wrong-doing shall surely earn salvation for they follow the right path. Such was the argument with which We furnished Abraham against his people. We raise whom We will to an exalted rank. Your Lord is Wise, All-Knowing. And We gave to him Isaac and Jacob; each one We guided as We had guided Noah before them. Among his progeny were David and Solomon, Job and Joseph, Moses and Aaron; thus We reward those who do good. And Zachariah and John, Jesus and Elias; each was of the Righteous. And Ishmael and Elisha, Jonah and Lot, each one We preferred above all beings, as We exalted their fathers, their offspring and their brethren; We elected them and guided them to a straight Path. Such is God's guidance. He bestows it on whom He pleases of His servants. But if they had served other gods besides Him, their labours would have been in vain. On them We bestowed the scriptures, wisdom and prophethood. If these are disbelieved by this generation, then We shall entrust them to others who are not disbelievers. These are the ones whom God guided. Follow their guidance, and say: 'I ask no wage for it; it is but a reminder to all beings.' (6:82-90).

Heaven and Hell

They underrate the might of God. But on the Day of Resurrection He will hold the entire earth in His grasp and fold up the skies in His right hand. Glory be to Him! Exalted be He above all that they associate with Him. The Trumpet shall be blown and whoever is in the heavens and whoever is on the earth shall swoom, save whom God wills. Then it shall be blown a second time and they will stand and look around them. The earth will shine with the light of its Lord and the Book will be set in place. The prophets and witnesses shall be brought in and all shall be judged with fairness: none shall be wronged. Each soul shall be paid in full for what it has wrought, for He is well-aware of what they do. Then the disbelievers will be driven into Hell in hordes. When they draw near, its gates will be opened, and its keepers will say to them: "Did not messengers come to you from among yourselves, reciting to you the signs of your Lord and warning you of the meeting of this day?" They shall say: "Yes, indeed." And thus the punishment which the unbelievers have been promised shall be fulfilled. It shall be said: "Enter the gates of Hell, to dwell therein forever." Evil is the dwelling-place of the arrogant. Then those who feared their Lord shall be led in bands into Paradise. When they draw near, its gates will be opened and its keepers shall say: "Peace be upon you! Well you have done. Enter Paradise and dwell therein forever." They will say: "Praise be to God, Who has been true to His promise to us and has made us inherit the land, that we may dwell wherever we wish in Paradise." Blessed is the reward of the righteous. And you will see the angels encircling about the Throne, hymning the praises of their Lord. Mankind will be judged with fairness and it will be said: "Praise be to God, Lord of the Worlds." (39:67-75).

Prayer

"I am God. There is no god but Me. So serve Me, and perform regular prayers for my remembrance." (20:14).

Perform the prayers at sunset, at nightfall and at dawn; the dawn prayer is witnessed. And pray for a part of the night, an additional duty for you; it may be that your Lord will raise you up to an honourable station (17:78-79).

Be constant in praying at the beginning and the end of the day, and in the night too. Good deeds make amends for sins. That is a reminder for the mindful. Therefore have patience; God will not deny the righteous their reward (11:114-115).

Be ever mindful of prayers, including the middle prayer. And stand obedient to God (2:238).

And when you have performed the prayer, remember God, standing, sitting and lying down. Then, when you are secure, perform the prayer, for prayer is a duty incumbent on the faithful, to be observed at appointed hours (4:103).

Recite what has been revealed to you of the Book, and perform the prayer; prayer prevents indecency and evil. God's remembrance is greatest of all. And God knows what you do (29:45).

Fasting

Believers, fasting is prescribed for you, as it was prescribed for those before you, so that you may ward off evil. Fast a certain number of days; but if any of you be sick or on a journey, let him fast a similar number of other days, and it is incumbent upon those who can afford it to make a sacrifice by feeding a needy person. He who does good of his own accord shall be well rewarded, but to fast is better for you, if you but knew it. In the month of Ramadan the Qur'an was revealed, a book of guidance for mankind with clear proofs of guidance distinguishing right from wrong. So those of you who witness the month should fast during it. But anyone who is sick or on a journey may fast a similar number of other days. God desires ease for you, not hardship. He desires you to fast the whole month so that you may magnify God for having guided you and He wishes you to render thanks (2:183-186).

Alms-giving

Believers, bestow in alms a part of that with which We have provided you, before there comes a day when there shall be neither trading, nor friendship nor intercession. Truly it is the unbelievers who are the wrongdoers (2:254).

He who spends his wealth in the way of God is like a grain of corn that sprouts seven ears, every ear bearing a hundred grains. God gives abundance to whom He wills; God is munificent and all-knowing. Those who spend their wealth in the way of God then do not follow up what they spend with reproaches and insults shall be rewarded by their Lord; they shall have nothing to fear or regret. A kind word with forgiveness is better than almsgiving followed by insults. God is self-sufficient and clement. Believers, do not mar your almsgiving with taunts and mischief-making, like those who spend their wealth only to be seen and praised by people, and believe neither in God nor in the Last Day. Such people are like a rock covered with a little earth; a shower falls upon it and leaves it hard and bare. They shall gain nothing from their works. God does not guide the unbelievers. But those who give away their wealth from a desire to please God and strengthen their souls are like a garden on a hillside; if a rainstorm falls upon it, it yields up twice its normal crop; and if no rain falls upon it, it is watered by the dew. God sees what you do. Would any of you, being a man well-advanced in age with helpless children to support, wish to have his garden—a garden planted with palm-trees, vines and all manner of fruits, and watered by running streams—blasted and consumed by a fiery whirlwind? Thus God makes plain to you His revelation, so that you may give thought. Believers, give in alms of the wealth you have lawfully earned and of that which We Have brought out of the earth for you; not of worthless things which you yourselves would only reluctantly accept. Know that God is self-sufficient and glorious. Satan threatens you with poverty and bids you to commit indecency. But God promises you His forgiveness and bounty. God is munificent and all-knowing. He gives wisdom to whom He wills; and whoever is granted wisdom receives great good. But none take heed except people of understanding (2:261-269).

Pilgrimage

Perform the pilgrimage and visit the Sacred House for God's sake. If you are prevented, send such offerings as you can afford, and do not shave your heads until the offerings have reached their destination. But if any of you is ill or suffers from an ailment of the head, he must pay a ransom, either by fasting or by almsgiving or by offering a sacrifice. In peacetime if any of you combines the visit with the pilgrimage, he must make such offerings as he can afford; but if he lacks the means, let him fast three days during the pilgrimage and seven when he has returned; that is, ten days in all. That is incumbent on one whose family are not present at the Holy Mosque. Have fear of God: know that He is stern in retribution. Make the pilgrimage in the appointed months. Whoever intends to perform it in those months must abstain from sexual intercourse, obscene language and acrimonious disputes while on pilgrimage. God is aware of whatever good you do. Provide yourselves well; the best provision is piety. Fear Me, then, you that are endowed with understanding. It is no offence for you to seek the bounty of your Lord by trading. When you press on from 'Arafat, remember God as you approach the Sacred Monument. Remember Him who gave you guidance when you were in error.

Then press on from where the pilgrims go out, and implore the forgiveness of God. He is forgiving and merciful. And when you have fulfilled your holy rites, remember God as you remember your fathers or yet more devoutly. There are some who say: "Lord, give us abundance in this world." These shall have no share in the world to come. But there are others who say: "Lord, give us what is good both in this world and in the next, and save us from the doom of Hell." These shall have a share of the reward. Swift is the reckoning of God. Remember God during the appointed days. He that departs on the second day incurs no sin, nor does he who stays longer, if he truly fears God. Have fear of God, then, and know that you shall be gathered before Him (2:196:203).

Sacrifice

For every nation We have appointed a holy rite that they may pronounce the name of God over the beasts which He has given them for food. Your God is One God; so surrender to Him. And give good news to the humble, whose hearts tremble with awe at the mention of God; who endure their misfortunes with fortitude, attend to their prayers and spend in charity of that which We have bestowed on them. And as for the sacrifice of cattle, We have ordained it for you as one of the symbols set up by God. They are of much use to you. So pronounce God's name over them as you draw them up in line and slaughter them; and when they have fallen down, eat of their flesh, and feed with it the poor person and the beggar. Thus We have subjected them to you so that you may be thankful. Their flesh and blood do not reach God; it is your piety that reaches Him. Thus He has subjected them to you, so that you may magnify God for having guided you. And give good news to the righteous (22:34-37).

&.

Serving God

To God belongs all that the heavens and the earth contain. Whether you reveal your thoughts or hide them, God will bring you to account for them. He will forgive whom He will and punish whom He will; He has power over all things. The Prophet believes in what has been revealed to him by his Lord and so do the faithful. They all believe in God and His angels, His scriptures and His prophets. We make no distinction between any of His prophets. They say: "We hear and We obey. Forgive us, Lord; to You we shall return." God does not charge a soul with more than it can bear. It shall be requited for whatever good and whatever evil it has done. "Lord do not take us to task if we forget or lapse into error. Lord, do not lay on us the burden You laid on those before us. Lord, do not charge us with more than we can bear. Pardon us, forgive us, and have mercy on us, You alone are our Protector. Help us against the unbelievers." (2:284-286).

The Shari'ah

The Lord has enjoined you to worship none but Him, and to show kindness to parents. If either or both of them reach old age with you, show them no sign of impatience, nor rebuke them; but speak kindly to them. Treat them with humility and tenderness and say: "Lord, be merciful to them even as they cherished and reared me when I was an infant." Your Lord knows best what is in your hearts; He knows if you are righteous. He is Forgiving to those who turn to Him again and again. Give to the near of kin their due, and also to the destitute and to the wayfarers. Do not squander your substance wastefully, for the wasteful are Satan's brothers; and Satan is ever ungrateful to his Lord. But if, while waiting for your Lord's bounty, you lack the means to assist them then at least speak to them kindly. Be neither miserly or prodigal, for then you should either be reproached or reduced to penury.

Your Lord gives abundantly to whom He wills and sparingly to whom He pleases. He knows and observes His servants. You shall not slay your children for fear of want. We will provide for them and for you. To kill them is a great sin. Do not commit adultery, for it is indecent and evil. Do not slay any person whom God has forbidden you to kill, except for a just cause. If someone is slain unjustly, to his heir We have given the right of retaliation. But let him not carry his vengeance too far, for his victim in turn will be assisted and avenged. Do not interfere with the property of orphans except with the best of motives, until they reach maturity. Keep your promises; you are accountable for all that you promise. Give full measure when you measure and weigh with even scales; that is fair and better in the end. Do not pursue what you do not know; man's eyes, ears and heart—each of his senses will be closely questioned. Do not walk on the earth with haughty self-conceit; you cannot cleave the earth, nor can you rival the mountains in stature. All this is evil and odious in the sight of your Lord. These injunctions are but a part of the wisdom with which your Lord has inspired you. Do not appoint another god with God, or you will be cast into Hell, despised and rejected (17:23-39).

The Servants
of the Merciful

The true servants of the Merciful are those who walk humbly upon the earth and say: "Peace!" to the ignorant who accost them: who pass the night standing and prostrate in adoration of their Lord; who say: "Lord ward off from us the punishment of Hell, for its punishment is everlasting, an evil dwelling and an evil resting-place"; who, when they spend, are neither wasteful nor niggardly, but keep the golden mean; who invoke no other god besides God, and do not kill save for a just cause; who do not commit adultery. He that does this shall meet with evil: his punishment shall be doubled on the Day of Resurrection and in disgrace he shall abide forever—unless he repent and believe and do good works, for then God will change his sins to good actions; God is Forgiving and Merciful: he that repents and does good works truly returns to God; who do not bear false witness and when they pass by idle talk, pass by with dignity; who do not turn a blind eye and a deaf ear to the revelations of their Lord when they are reminded of them; who say: "Lord, give us joy in our spouses and offspring, and make us examples to those who are God-fearing." These shall be rewarded with the highest heaven for their patient endurance. There they shall be welcomed with a greeting and peace, and there they shall abide forever; a blessed dwelling and a blessed resting place (25:63-76).

$$\clubsuit$$

Trust in God

There is but one God. In Him let the believers put their trust. Believers, you have an enemy in your spouses and children: beware of them. But if you overlook their offences and forgive and pardon them, then know that God is Forgiving and Merciful. Your wealth and your children are but a temptation. God's reward is great. Therefore fear Him with all your hearts and be attentive, obedient and charitable for the good of your own selves; for those who guard themselves from their own avarice will surely prosper. If you give God a generous loan, He will repay you twofold and will forgive you, for God is Ever Responsive to gratitude and is Most Forbearing (64:13-18).

Words of Wisdom

Luqman admonished his son: "My son," he said, "do not associate others with God; to associate other with God is a mighty wrong." We have enjoined man to show kindness to his parents, for with much pain his mother bears him, and he is not weaned before he is two years of age. Give thanks to Me and to your parents. To Me all things shall return. But if they press you to associate others with Me, of whom you know nothing, then then do not obey them. Be kind to them in this world, but follow the way of him who turns to me. To me you shall return and I shall tell you what you have done. "My dear son, God will bring all things to light, be they as small as a grain of mustard seed, be they hidden inside a rock or in heaven or on earth. God is Wise and All-Knowing. My dear son, be steadfast in prayer, enjoin good and forbid evil. Endure with fortitude whatever befalls you. That is true constancy. Do not treat people with scorn, nor walk haughtily on the earth; God does not love the arrogant and the vainglorious. Rather let your gait be modest and your voice be low; the ugliest of all voices is the braying of the ass" (31:13-19).

God-Fearing People

They ask you about the spoils. Say: "The spoils belong to God and the Messenger. So fear God and settle your disputes. Obey God and His Messenger, if you are true believers." The true believers are those whose hearts tremble with awe at the mention of God, and whose faith grows stronger as they listen to His revelations. They put their trust in their Lord, pray steadfastly, and give in alms from that which We have given them. Such are the true believers. They shall be exalted and forgiven by their Lord, and a generous provision shall be made for them (8:1-4).

The Good Life

God enjoins justice, kindness and charity to one's kindred, and forbids indecency, abomination and oppression. He admonishes you so that you may take heed. Keep faith with God when you make a covenant with Him. Do not break your oaths after having confirmed them and having called upon God to be your surety. God has knowledge of all your actions. Do not, like the woman who unravels the thread which she has firmly spun, take oaths with mutual deceit and break them on finding yourselves superior to others in numbers. In this God puts you to the proof. On the Day of Resurrection He will make clear to you that over which you are at variance. Had God willed, He would have united you into one community. But He leaves in error whom He wills and guides whom He wills. You shall be questioned about your actions. Do not take oaths to deceive each other, lest your foot should slip after it has stood firm, and lest evil should befall you for debarring others from the path of God, and lest there should await you a mighty punishment.

Do not sell the covenant of God for a trifling price. His reward is better then all your gain, if you but knew it. Your worldly riches are transitory, but God's reward is everlasting. We shall reward the steadfast according to their noblest deeds. Be they men or women, those who believe and do what is right We shall surely endow with a good life; We shall reward them according to their noblest actions (16:90-97).

Haram and Halal
(Lawful and Unlawful)

Say: "Come, I will tell you what your Lord has made binding on you: that you ascribe no partner to Him: that you show kindness to your parents; that you do not slay your children because of poverty; We provide for you and for them; that you do not commit any shameful deeds, openly or secretly; that you do not slay the soul God has prohibited except by right. Thus God exhorts you, so that you may grow in wisdom." Do not touch the property of orphans, but strive to improve their lot until they reach maturity. Give just weight and full measure; We never charge a soul with more than it can bear. When you speak, be just, even though it be against a relative. Be true to God's covenant. Thus God exhorts you, so that you may take heed (6:151-152).

Say: "My Lord has forbidden all shameful deeds, whether overt or disguised, and sin and wrongful oppression; or associate with God that for which no warrant has been revealed, or to tell of God what you do not know. Every nation has its term; when their hour comes, they shall not put it back by a single hour nor put it forward. Children of Adam, when apostles of your own come to proclaim to you My revelations, those that take warning and mend their ways will have nothing to fear or to regret; but those that deny and scorn Our revelations shall be inhabitants of the Fire, and there they shall remain forever (7:33-36).

Heavenly Souls

Indeed man was born with a restless disposition. When evil befalls him he is filled with self-pity, but blessed with good fortune he grows niggardly. Not so the worshippers who are steadfast in their prayer; who set aside a due portion of their goods for the needy and the dispossessed; who truly believe in the Day of Reckoning and dread the punishment of their Lord (for none is secure from the punishment of God); who preserve their chastity (save with their wives and slave girls, for in their case they are not blameworthy; but those who lust after other than those are transgressors); who keep their trusts and promises and bear true witness; and who attend to their prayers. These shall be laden with honours, and shall dwell in fair Gardens. (70:19-35).

The Serene Soul

As for man, when his Lord tests him by honouring him and bestowing favours on him, he says: "My Lord has honoured me." But when He tests him by straitening his means of life, he says: "My Lord despises me." No! But you show no kindness to the orphan, and do not urge one another to feed the poor. Greedily you devour the inheritance of the weak, and you love riches with all your hearts. No! But when the earth is crushed to fine dust, and your Lord comes, and the angels rank on rank, and Hell is brought near, on that Day man will take heed but what good will it do him now? He will say: "Would that I had sent before me some provision for my life." But on that Day none will punish as He will punish, nor will any bind with chains like His. Serene soul, return to your Lord, well-pleased and pleasing Him. Join My servants and enter My Paradise (89:15-30).

Divine Souls

Believers, do not live on usury, doubling your wealth many times over. Have fear of God and you shall prosper. Guard yourselves against the fire of Hell prepared for unbelievers. Obey God and the Prophet, so that you may find mercy. Vie with each other to earn the forgiveness of your Lord and a Paradise as vast as heaven and earth, prepared for the righteous; those who give alms alike in prosperity and in adversity; who curb their anger and forgive their fellow men. God loves the charitable. And who, if they commit evil or wrong their souls, remember God and seek forgiveness for their sins—who but God forgives sins—and do not knowingly persist in their misdeeds. These shall be rewarded with forgiveness from their Lord and Gardens underneath which running streams flow, where they shall dwell forever. Blessed is the reward of those who do good works. (3:130-136).

The Correct Way

That which you have been given is but the fleeting comfort of this life. For better and more enduring is God's reward to those who believe and put their trust in Him; who avoid gross sins and indecencies and, when angered, are willing to forgive; who respond to the call of their Lord, are constant in prayer, and conduct their affairs by mutual consent; who bestow in alms a portion of that which We have given them and, when oppressed, seek to redress their wrongs. Let evil be rewarded with like evil. But he who forgives and seeks reconcilement shall be rewarded by God. He does not love the wrongdoers. Those who avenge themselves when wronged incur no guilt. But great is the guilt of those who oppress their fellow men and conduct themselves with wickedness and injustice in the land. These shall be sternly punished. But true constancy lies in forgiveness and patient forbearance (42:36-43).

Profitable Trading

Believers, shall I point out to you a profitable course that will save you from a painful doom? Believe in God and His Messenger and strive for His cause with your wealth and your lives. That would be best for you, if you only knew it. He will forgive you your sins and admit you to Gardens, underneath which running streams flow; He will lodge you in pleasant mansions in the Gardens of Eden. That is the supreme triumph. And He will bestow upon you other blessings which you desire: help from God and a speedy victory. Give the good news to the faithful. Believers, be God's helpers. When Jesus, the son of Mary, said to his disciples: "Who will help me on the way to God?" They replied: "We are God's helpers." Then some of the Israelites believed in him while others did not. We helped the believers against their enemies and they triumphed over them (61:10-14).

Real Piety

Piety does not consist in turning your faces towards the east or the west. The pious are those who believe in God and in the Last Day, in the angels and the scriptures and the prophets; who for the love of God give their wealth to kinsfolk, orphans, the poor, wayfarers in need and beggars, and for the redemption of captives; who attend to their prayers and pay the poor-due; who are true to their promises and endure with fortitude misfortune, hardships and peril. These are the true believers, these are the God-fearing (2:177).

God's Hospitality

Do the unbelievers think that they can make My servants protectors against Me? We have prepared Hell to be their dwelling place. Say: "Shall we tell you who will lose most through their labours? Those whose endeavours in this world are misguided and who think even then that what they do is right; who disbelieve the revelations of their Lord and deny that they will ever meet Him." Vain are their works. On the Day of Resurrection We shall not honour them. Hell is their reward: because they had no faith and scoffed at My messengers and My signs. As for those who have faith and do good works, the Gardens of Paradise shall be their abode. They shall dwell there forever, desiring no change to befall them. Say: "If all the sea were ink with which to write the words of my Lord, the sea would surely be consumed before my Lord's words were finished, though we brought another sea to replenish it." Say: "I am but a mortal like yourselves. It is revealed to me that your Lord is One God. Let those that hope to meet their Lord do what is right and make none sharer of the worship due to his Lord." (18:102-110).

The Believer's Livelihood

Believers, when you are summoned to Friday prayer, hasten to the remembrance of God and cease your trading. That would be best for you, if you but knew it. Then, when the prayer is ended, disperse and go your ways in quest of God's bounty. Remember God always, so that you may prosper. But when they see some merchandise or passing delight, they flock to it eagerly, leaving you[1] alone. Say: "That which God has

---

1. The Prophet

in store is far better than and passing delight or merchandise. God is the best of providers." (62:9-11).

The People of Paradise

Truly successful are the believers who are humble in their prayers; who avoid profanity, and are active in charitable works; who restrain their carnal desires, (except with their wives and slavegirls, for these are lawful to them; whoever seeks after more than that has transgressed); who are true to their trusts and promises and never neglect their prayers. These are the inheritors of Paradise, and therein they shall abide forever (23:1-11).

Everything for God

God has bought from the believers their selves and their possessions and in return has promised them Paradise. They fight for His cause, slay, and are slain. That is a promise binding upon God in the Torah, the Gospel and the Qur'an. And who is more true to His promise than God? Rejoice, then, in the bargain you have made. That is the supreme triumph. Those who repent, those who worship, those who praise Him, those who journey, those who bow down, those who prostrate themselves, those who enjoin right, forbid wrong, and observe the commandments of God, shall be richly rewarded. Give the good news to the believers (9:111-112).

❦

The Believer is God's Tree

Do you not see how God compares a good word to a good tree? Its root is firm and its branches are in the sky; it yields its fruit in every season by God's leave. God gives people parables so that they may take heed. But an evil word is like an evil tree torn out of the earth, possessing no stability. God will strengthen the faithful with His steadfast Word, both in this life and the hereafter. He leads the wrongdoers astray. He accomplishes what He pleases (14:24-27).

Good Advice

God commands you to hand back your trusts to their rightful owners, and to pass judgement upon people with fairness. Noble is the advice God gives you. He hears all and observes all (4:58).

He who fears God will take heed, but the most sinner will flout the warning. He shall be cast into the great Fire, where he shall neither die nor live. Successful is he who purifies himself, who remembers the name of his Lord and prays. Yet you[1] prefer the life of this world, although the life to come is better and more lasting (87:10-17).

Doomed
to Destruction

Woe to every backbiting slanderer who amasses riches and sedulously hoards them, thinking that his riches will render him immortal! By no means! He shall be flung to the Destroying torment. Would that you knew what the Destroying torment was like! It is

---

1. The unbelievers of Mecca

Gods' own kindled fire, which will rise up to people's hearts. It will close upon them from every side, in endless columns (104:1-9).

The Deniers
of God's Signs

He who turns away from My remembrance shall live in anguish and come before Us blind on the Day of Resurrection. "Lord", he will say, "why have you brought me blind before you, when in my lifetime I was blessed with sight?" God will answer: "Because Our signs came to you and you forgot them. In like manner this Day you are yourself forgotten." And thus do We reward the transgressor who denies the revelations of his Lord. But the punishment of the world to come is more terrible and more lasting (20:124-127).

Fair Testimony

Believers, be ever steadfast in your devotion to God, bearing fair testimony. Do not allow hatred for some people to turn you away from justice. Deal justly; justice is nearer to piety. Have fear of God; He knows what you do. God has promised those who believe and do good works forgiveness and a rich reward. And the unbelievers who deny Our signs shall dwell in Hell (5:8-10).

Living in Harmony

Believers, when you confront an opposing force, stand firm and make constant mention of God, so that you may triumph. Obey God and His Messenger and do not quarrel with one another, lest you should lose courage and your resolve weaken. Have patience; God is with those who are patient. Do not be like those who left their homelands elated with arrogance and a desire to be seen and praised by men. They debar others from the path of God: but God encompasses what they do (8:45-47).

Islamic Society

Believers, if an ungodly person brings you some news, inquire first into its truth, lest you should hurt others un wittingly and, afterwards, be filled with remorse for what you have done. Know that God's Messenger is among you. If he obeyed you in many matters, you would surely come to grief. But God has endeared the Faith to you and beautified it in your hearts, making unbelief, wrongdoing and disobedience abhorrent to you. Such are those who are rightly guided through God's grace and blessing. God is wise and all-knowing. If two parties of the believers take up arms against one another, make peace between them. If either of them commits aggression against the other, fight against the aggressors until they submit to God's judgement. When they submit, make peace between them in equity and justice; God loves the just. The believers are one brotherhood; make peace among your brothers and fear God, so that you may be shown mercy. Believers, let no men mock other men who may perhaps be better than themselves. Let no women mock other women, who may perhaps be better than themselves. Do not defame one another, nor call one another by nicknames. It is evil to be called by a bad name after embracing the true faith. Those who do not repent are wrongdoers. Believers, avoid immoderate suspicion, for in some cases suspicion is a sin. Do not spy on one another, nor backbite one another. Would any of you like to eat the flesh of his dead brother? Surely you would loathe it. Have fear of God. He is forgiving and merciful. Mankind, We have created you from a male and a female and divided you into nations and tribes, so that you may know one another. The noblest of you in God's sight is the one who fears God most. God is wise, and all-knowing (49:6-13).

Calling to God

Call people to the way of your Lord with wisdom and kindly exhortation. Argue with them in the most courteous manner. Your Lord knows best those who stray from His path and those who are rightly guided. If you punish, let your punishment be proportionate to the wrong that has been done to you. But it is best for you to endure your wrong with patience. So be patient; your patience is for God. Do not grieve over the unbelievers, and neither be distressed by their plots. God is with those who keep from evil and do good works. (16:125-128).

Magnifying the Lord

You who are wrapped up in your vestment, arise and give warning, Magnify your Lord, purify your inner self. Keep away from all pollution. Be patient, for your Lord's sake. The day when the trumpet sounds should not be an easy one for the unbelievers; it shall be a day of anguish for them (74:1-10).

No, by the moon! By the departing night and the rising dawn, Hell is a dire scourge, a warning to mankind; alike to those of you who would advance and those who would hang back. Each soul is the hostage of its own deeds. But those on the right hand—they will be in their gardens, inquiring of the sinners; "What brought you into the Fire?" They will reply: "We never prayed or fed the hungry. We engaged in vain disputes and denied the Day of Reckoning until death overtook us." No intercessor's plea shall avail them then (74:32-48).

Eternity is Better

S uccessful is the person who purifies himself, who remembers the name of his Lord, and prays. Yet you[1] prefer this life, although the life to come is better and more lasting. All this is written in earlier scriptures; the scriptures of Abraham and Moses (87:14-19).

Their Efforts will be Rewarded

W e have created man from a drop of thickened fluid so that We may test him. We made him a being endowed with hearing and sight. We have shown him the way, whether he be grateful or ungrateful. For the unbelievers We have prepared fetters and chains, and a blazing fire. But the righteous shall drink a cup flavoured with the Camphor—a spring at which the servants of God will refresh themselves as it gushes forth abundantly; they who keep their vows and dread

---

1. The unbelievers of Mecca

the far-spread terrors of Judgement Day; who, though they hold it dear, give sustenance to the poor person, the orphan and the captive, saying: 'We feed you for God's sake alone; we seek of you neither recompense nor thanks; for we fear from Him a day of anguish and of woe." God will deliver them from the evil of that day, and will make their faces shine with joy. He will reward them for their steadfastness with robes of silk and the delights of Paradise. Reclining there upon soft couches, they shall feel neither the scorching heat not the biting cold. Trees will spread their shade around them, and fruit will hang in clusters over them. They shall be served with silver dishes, and beakers as large as goblets; silver goblets which they themselves shall measure; and cups brimful with ginger-flavoured water from the Fount of Selsabil. They shall be attended by boys graced with eternal youth, who, to the beholder's eyes will seem like sprinkled pearls. When you gaze upon that scene you will behold a kingdom blissful and glorious. They shall be arrayed in garments of fine green silk and rich brocade, and adorned with bracelets of silver. Their Lord will give them pure nectar to drink. Thus you shall be rewarded; since your endeavours in life shall be pleasing to God. (76:2-22).

The Day of Reward and Retribution

When the sky is cleft asunder; when the stars scatter and the oceans burst beyond their bounds; when the graves are overturned; each soul will know what it has sent ahead and it has left behind. O man! What evil has enticed you away from your gracious Lord who created you, gave you an upright form, and well-proportioned you? In whatever shape He willed, He moulded you. Yet, you deny the Last Judgement. Surely there are guardians watching over you, noble recorders who know of all your actions. The righteous shall surely dwell in Bliss. But the wicked shall burn in a blazing fire on the Judgement-Day; which they shall not be able to evade. Would that you knew what the Day of Judgement is! Oh, would that you knew what the Day of Judgement is! A Day when no soul shall be of the least avail to another soul; for on that Day all sovereignty is God's alone (82:1-19).

The Religion
That is Pleasing to God

As for the home of the world to come, We shall grant it to those who seek neither to exalt themselves in this world nor to spread corruption. The righteous shall have a blessed end. Whoever does good shall be rewarded with what is better. But those who do evil shall be requited only according to what they did (28:83-84).

As for him who rebelled, and preferred the life of this world; Hell shall be his Final Abode. But as for him who feared to stand before his Lord and restrained his soul from base desires; Paradise shall be his Final Abode (79:37-41).

He that chooses a religion other than Islam, it will not be accepted from him and in the world to come he will be one of the lost (3:85).

Prayers

Praise be to God, Lord of Creation, the Beneficent, the Merciful, King of Judgement Day. You alone we worship, and to You alone we pray for help. Guide us to the straight path, the path of those whom You have favoured, not of those who have incurred Your wrath, nor of those who have gone astray (I:1-7).

To the Lord

Lord, do not take us not to task if we forget or lapse into error. Lord, do not lay on us the burden You laid on those before us. Lord, do not charge us with more than we can bear. Pardon us, forgive us our sins, and have mercy upon us. You alone are our Protector. Give us victory over the deniers (2:286).

God, Lord of all sovereignty, You bestow sovereignty on whom You will and take it away from whom You please; You exalt whomever You will and abase whomever You please. In Your hand lies all that is good; You have power over all things. You cause the night to pass into the day and the day to pass into the night; You bring forth the living from the dead and the dead from the living. You give without stint to whom You will (3:26-27).

Protect Us!

L ord, give us joy in our spouses and offspring, and cause us to be foremost among those who are God-fearing (25:74).

Inspire me, Lord, to render thanks for the favours You have bestowed on me and on my parents, and to do good work that will please You. Admit me, through Your mercy, among your righteous servants (27:19).

Lord, Your mercy and knowledge embrace all things. Forgive those that repent and follow Your path. Shield them from the scourge of Hell. Admit them, Lord, to the Gardens of Eden which You have promised them, together with all the righteous among their fathers, their spouses, and their descendents. You are the Almighty, the Wise One. Deliver them from all evil. He whom You will deliver from evil on that Day is surely one You have graced with Your mercy. That is the supreme triumph (40:7-9).

Help Us!

Lord, give us what is good both in this world and in the next and save us from the chastisement of the Fire (2:201).

Lord, fill our hearts with steadfastness. Make firm our step and help us against the unbelievers (2:250).

Lord, do not cause our hearts to go astray after You have guided us. Grant us Your own mercy; You are the munificent Giver (3:8).

Lord, we believe in You: forgive us our sins and keep us from the torment of Hell-fire (3:16).

Purify Our Hearts

Forgive us, Lord, and forgive our brothers who embraced the Faith before us. Do not put in our hearts any malice towards the faithful. Lord, You are compassionate, and merciful (59:10).

Lord, in You we have put our trust; to You we turn and to You we shall come at last. Lord, do not expose us to the designs of the unbelievers. Forgive us, Lord;

You are the Mighty, the Wise One (60:4-5).

Lord, perfect our light for us and forgive us. You have power over all things (66:8).

Grant Us a Righteous End

Lord, You have not created this in vain. Glory be to You! Save us from the torment of Hell-fire. Lord, those whom You will cast into Hell shall be put to eternal shame: none will help the wrongdoers. Lord, we have heard a crier calling men to the true Faith, saying: "Believe in your Lord." So we believed. Lord, then, forgive us our sins and remove from us our evil deeds and make us die with the righteous. Lord, grant us what You promised through your messengers, and do not cast shame on us on the Day of Resurrection. Truely, You never fail to fulfil Your promise (3:191-194).

Have Mercy on Us!

L ord, make me and my descendents steadfast in prayer. Lord, accept my prayer. Forgive me, Lord, and forgive my parents and all the faithful on the Day of Reckoning (14:40-41).

Lord, have mercy on them both (i.e., my parents) as they cherished and cared for me when I was a little child (17:24).

Save us from Evil

L ord, we have wronged our souls. Pardon us and have mercy on us, or we shall surely be among the lost (7:23).

Lord, bless us with patience and let us die as Muslims (who have surrendered themselves to Your Will) (7:126).

Lord, You alone are our Guardian. Forgive us and have mercy on us: You are the Best of those who forgive. Ordain for us what is good, both in this life and in the Hereafter. To You alone we have turned in repentance (7:155-156).

Lord, do not let us suffer at the hands of the

wicked. Deliver us, through Your mercy, from the unbelievers (10:85-86).

Creator of the heavens and earth, You are my Guardian in this world and in the next. Let me die as one submitting to Your Will (i.e., Muslim) and join the righteous (12:101).

Strengthen Us!

Lord, grant me a goodly entrance and a goodly exit, and sustain me with Your power. (17:80).

Lord, have mercy on us and guide us out of our ordeal.

Do Not Leave Me Alone!

Lord, put courage into my heart, and ease my task for me. Free my tongue from its impediment, so that they may understand my speech (20:25-28).

Lord, cause me to grow in knowledge (20:114).

Lord, I have been afflicted with distress: but You are the Most Merciful of all who show mercy (21:83).

Lord, do not leave me childless; You are the Best of all heirs (21:89).

Lord, let my landing from this ark be blessed. You alone can make me land in safety. (23:29).

Lord, build me a house with You in Paradise (66:11).

Lord, I stand in need of the blessing which You have sent me (28:24).

Lord, deliver me from these corrupt people (29:30).

Avenge me, Lord, I am overcome! (54:10).

Save Us From Doom

Lord, I seek refuge in You from the promptings of the devils. Lord, I seek refuge in You from their presence (23:98-99).

Lord, we believe in You. Forgive us and have mercy on us; You are the Most Merciful (23:109).

Lord, ward off from us the punishment of Hell, for its punishment is everlasting (25:65).

PART FOUR

The Garden of Paradise

Belief in God

God is the source of all goodness. He can be seen everywhere in the universe. His power is evident in the form of light and heat. He converts matter into greenery and flowing water. His glory is made manifest in colour, taste and fragrance. Motion and magnetism are evidence of His strength.

Belief in a God of such supreme perfection is more than just a dogma. It illuminates man's soul and enraptures his heart. If one relishes a delicious fruit, and goes into ecstasy on hearing a tuneful melody, how then can one fail to be moved by the discovery of God, who is the fountainhead of all goodness.

When one truly discovers God, He becomes like a fragrance which one savours, a delicious taste which one relishes, a spectacle which captivates one's vision, a melody which never ceases to thrill. God has created all these exquisite delights: His Being is their treasure house. Drawing close to God is like entering paradise. It is like dwelling in a garden of exquisite beauty and fragrance, or being close to the source of all light.

Discovery of God

God's true servant is one who is thrown into such spiritual excitement by the discovery of God that he always has God in his thoughts. The beholding of God in all His majesty inspires such awe and fear in him that the hair of his body stands on end. One who finds God fears and loves Him above all else. His entire attention is focused on God alone.

When he reads the Qur'an, he is overwhelmed with gratitude to God for having guided him, thus saving him from the darkness of ignorance. When he considers the life-pattern of the holy Prophet, his whole being is thankful to God for having provided man with such an impeccable example of how life should be lived, and having then preserved that model for all time. When he prostrates himself in worship, he feels as if God has embraced him in His mercy. When he eats, every fibre of his being thanks God for the nourishment and sustenance with which He has provided man. When he drinks water, tears of thanks flow from his eyes, for if God had not provided water, how would he be able to quench his thirst?

God's Neighbour

One who has discovered God becomes close to God even in this world. His spirit is bathed in the light of God. If even the sight of flowers arouses finer feelings in a person, how can one discover God and not be moved to a state of sublime ecstasy?

Many people claim to be close to God, but are still in fact a long way from Him. They speak of God, but their actions show that they have not even recognized their Lord.

They take God's name, but have not tasted the sweetness of the name which they utter. They claim to have found God, but have not experienced the fragrance of His garden. They display religious fervour in public, but there are no signs of their souls being illuminated with the light of God. They consider that God's paradise is reserved exclusively for them, but their lives are not touched by a heavenly breeze.

A strange God it must be who does not cause any vibration in one's thoughts. A strange heaven it must be to which people who show no reflection of the heavenly in their words and deeds will be automatically admitted. A strange hereafter it must be which will be inherited for all eternity by people who did not seek life-everlasting and were interested only in ephemeral pleasures.

It is regrettable that there are people who claim to have found God while in truth they have not found Him at all.

Spiritual Nourishment

A believer derives spiritual nourishment from the whole universe; he will partake of the same nourishment in material form in paradise. When zephyrs caress his body in this world, he feels as if he is being stroked by a divine hand. He beholds God's unfathomable mercy in the flowing motion of rivers. The chirping of birds inspires him to sing songs of divine praise. Whoever is granted such vision as comes with true belief sees evidence of God's glory in all things.

A tree is just a simple wooden structure, but what beautiful flowers blossom on it. Dry wood, growing on dry land, suddenly undergoes a silent transformation. Its branches burgeon with luxuriant blooms.

This happens so that, just by gazing at such a spectacle, one may feel inspired to cry out to God: "Lord, I too am like a piece of wood; only You can make me flower. I am like a barren stalk; only You can make me blossom and thrive. I am just an insignificant being; only You can put meaning into my life. I am standing on the verge of Hell; only You can enable me to enter paradise. I am far from You; only You can reach out and take me under Your protection."

Closeness to God

Only those who have recognized God in this world will be admitted to God's paradise in the next. The discoverer of God is one who sees God with conviction, despite the fact that in this world God is invisible; who hears God speaking to him with each throb of his heart; who reads the Book of God with a feeling that the pages of his own nature are being unfolded.

The discoverer of God is one whose moribund spirit has been quickened by faith; whose heart has been purified by remembrance of God; who proceeds by the light of God; whose heart trembles at the very mention of God's name; who receives God with tears and whose whole being surrenders to Him.

Whoever is close to God is close to heaven. Closeness to God begins in this world and culminates in the next. A person who experiences closeness to God feels that he is seeing an unseen reality. He feels very close to the most distant of Beings. He engages in conversation with One who does not seem to be present. He showers his affection on the most awesome of Beings. He establishes direct contact with the One who cannot be approached through any intermediary.

Paradise— The Greatest of Gifts

Everything in heaven and on earth bows to God, but no natural act of prostration can compare to man's obeisance. Other creatures submit to God involuntarily. Man does so expressly, of his own free will.

Man submits to God consciously and independently. No action in the world can compare with man's submission. Herein lies the real value of man. Man is the only creature who is fully aware of his total helplessness in the face of God's omnipotence. He counts himself as nothing and God as everything. He renounces his own ego in the face of divinity. He forsakes all power and surrenders totally to God. He controls his speech for God's sake, as if he had no tongue of his own.

Becoming a true believer is the greatest thing that can happen in the world. The reward for such belief must be similarly great. Heaven is the name of that reward. Paradise is not the price of one's actions: it is the gift of God. It is granted to those who offer God something which nothing else in the universe has offered. Accordingly, it is a gift which He has granted to no other creature.

Heavenly Vision

All of God's creation is so astounding that, were man to behold it, he would be lost in admiration of its absolute perfection. The face of the Creator is reflected in the wonders of His creation. But we have seen so much of the world that our senses have been dulled. We have become so familiar with the world around us that we fail to marvel at it as we should. Water, birds and trees—indeed everything in nature—is too wonderful for words. Everything is a reflection of the Creator. But we cannot see how amazing it all is. We are too familiar with it all.

In this man is being tested. It is for him to perceive extraordinary qualities in ordinary things. If one gazes at the world in awe, one will feel God's presence everywhere. One will live on earth as if one was face to face with God.

To behold God and to feel His immanence is the greatest discovery man can make in this world. If one is blessed with heavenly vision, one will perceive the light of God in rays of sunlight. The spectacle of trees will portray to one the countenance of God. One will feel God's touch in every gentle breeze. When one lays one's forehead on the ground in prostration one will feel as if one has cast oneself at God's feet. God is everywhere, but only those fortunate ones who have been blessed with heavenly vision can behold him.

God's Worshippers

Only one who has really been in love with someone can be moved to tears by the memory of his beloved. If one feels no attachment for someone, one cannot, simply because some occasion calls for it, force oneself to cry for that person.

Some adopt an attitude of humility towards their fellow men, while others remain arrogant. Some are fair and just, others oppress and persecute their fellows. Some are humble, others are proud. Some submit to the truth, others do not. People of such opposing attitudes cannot both worship God in a similar fashion. Only the first category of people will be genuinely humble in their worship. The second category may adopt the humble postures of worship—as the occasion demands—but they cannot thereby become God's humble servants. Humility in one's worship stems from a life of humility. One who is not humble in the totality of his existence cannot then be truly humble in his worship.

Those who truly worship God will enter paradise. They are the ones who serve God at all times, not just at specified times of worship. Paradise is an abode of truth. It has been prepared specially for those who are true in their worship. Those who are insincere will never be admitted to such an abode.

A Complete World

The pleasures of this world are short-lived. Its beauty soon fades from our vision. How much man longs for worldly honour and happiness, but before he has even begun to savour them, they begin to dwindle away to nothing. The world has everything that man wants, but it is not possible for anyone - even those who seem to have everything in life - to achieve all that they desire. Happiness is not necessarily the lot of the successful.

Man, as a being, is perfect, but his world is tragically imperfect. His life is meaningless until he inherits a world free of all limitations and disadvantages.

As a compensation for the incompleteness of this world, God has given us paradise. But gaining entry to it will be no easy matter. The price that has to be paid for an after-life of perfection is living through the present world of imperfection and being able to sacrifice this world for the next. This is the only way to enter paradise. Those who are not able to make this sacrifice will also enter an eternal world after death, but it will be a world of anguish and despair as opposed to one of joy and bliss.

Light After Darkness

Morning follows night. That which was concealed in darkness is revealed in the light of day. This is a sign of what is to come.

The light of eternity will tear the veils which have concealed the realities of human existence in the world. Everyone will appear in his true light. It will become clear who among us was masquerading as an ideal human being, while acting solely on baser animal instincts. It will become clear who was only paying lip service to righteousness. It will become clear who was falsely claiming to be a servant of God.

The truth about many others will also be revealed on that day. People will realize the true importance of those whom they used to rate poorly. Those who were never honoured in world gatherings will find honour among the angels. Those who were rejected by men will be accepted by God. Those who were wrongly accused of impiety in the world will be hailed for their piety in the presence of the Almighty.

When all Things Come to Light

The cosmos is full of meaning. It accepts nothing which is contrary to its nature and is not in accord with its design. Yet man wreaks evil and indulges in corruption on this our earth, the most fertile and exquisite portion of the universe. Truth is trampled upon in the name of progress and the cosmos, despite its meaningfulness, stands by in silence. It does not condemn the evil which is openly committed on earth. It does not proclaim truth and falsehood for what they are.

Does the cosmos contradict itself? Is it incapable of expressing itself? There are birds who sing melodiously, but is there no cosmic voice to proclaim the truth? There is, certainly, but God has silenced the voice of truth until the resurrection of man. When man rises from the dead, all things will testify to the truth. The whole universe will bear witness to the truth, and will give evidence before God. Justice will prevail. People will then realize that just as the cosmos possessed a sun to convert night into day, it also possessed a means of bringing to light such deeds as had remained concealed in obscurity.

Those who had rebelled on earth will pay in full for their rebellion; they will be cast into the fire of Hell. Those who had served God will be rewarded for their righteousness; God will be merciful to them. They will be admitted to heaven, where they will enjoy an everlasting life of honour and content.

A Dream World

God has created man with innumerable desires and longings. The means exist in this world for the fulfillment of his desires, but even so, man is unable to fulfill them. Sometimes old age intervenes and sometimes man's inherent limitations prevent him from achieving what he wishes; sometimes he is hindered by some weakness and sometimes he is not favoured by fortune.

Is man fated to come into the world with all sorts of desires and then leave the world, disappointed at having achieved none of them? This is not the case: God has prepared a paradise for man where he will be granted all that he desires. After death man enters into a complete world, a world free of all defects. He will find there everything that he had longed for on earth but had been unable to obtain.

Heaven after death is for those fortunate ones who live righteous lives on earth; who prove by their noble actions that they deserve an equally noble reward. Man will find in the next life the dream world which eludes him on earth. Only those who have paid the price in this life will deserve heaven in the next.

Loss Turned to Gain

Man longs more than anything for a world full of happiness. This longing is inborn in every human being, but everyone leaves the world with only a partial sense of fulfillment. Man wants to see all his desires satisfied in this world, but the world cannot provide what he wants; so he is left in a state of disillusionment.

We may build for ourselves the kind of home we have always dreamed of having but, in it, we are still beset by the rivalry, jealousy, enmity and vengeance of others. We make huge advances in the field of technology, only to see them rendered meaningless by new problems. Then, while we are still on the road to success, death puts an end to everything.

Man is quite right to long for an ideal world, but he can never find it on earth. He will have to wait until the next life for the realization of such a world. Faith in eternity invests our life on earth with meaning. Our life on earth is one of struggle, but in eternity, we will be rewarded for our efforts on earth. If one considers this world the ultimate destination, one is bound to be disappointed; but if one looks ahead to the Hereafter, then a world of eternal contentment opens out before one.

In a world where we seem bound to lose, only a faith which tells us the secret of turning our losses into gains can be the true one.

Avoiding Disaster

Man works hard to build a solid financial base for his life. When he builds a fine house for himself, he feels that his efforts have been rewarded. He builds success for himself in the world. Then suddenly death overtakes him. He leaves his home for the grave. His fine body is devoured by earth and worms. His worldly gain comes to nothing, as if there had been no connection between him and his achievements.

He dreamt of mansions in the world; now he has to enter the grave. Finally he is raised from the dead and brought before the Lord to be judged. There he will be absolutely destitute. He will not even have clothes to cover his body. Everything he had earned will amount to nothing. His friends will desert him. He will be left powerless. He will be deprived of all the supports which made him so sure of himself on earth.

It is an ill-fated journey on which one meets disaster as one nears one's destination. It is a strange traveller who thinks that he is heading towards his goal, and only realizes that he has been on the wrong track all along as he nears his destination.

§.

The Universal Way

The whole universe has submitted to God. Everything proceeds on the path that God has laid down for it. Trees stand high, but they cast their shadows on the ground in humility. Winds blow, but they do not clash with anybody. The sun radiates light on all alike; it does not discriminate between the weak and the mighty. Rain falls from the sky, benefiting all whom it reaches; it is not prejudiced against anyone. Birds and ants are busy in their search for their food, but they do not steal one another's share.

This is the path ordained by God for the universe, and this is the way that man should live also. God's beloved servants are humble like the shadow of a tree. They pass one another by like gentle puffs of wind. They are kind and well-meaning to one and all alike in the manner of the rain. They nourish others like river-water. They shed light on all like the sun. They are always careful not to trouble anyone.

Such pure souls will dwell in heaven. The people of heaven will live with one another like flowers in a garden. They will exude fragrance and will converse with one another in gentle tones. They will meet with one another like gentle breezes. How extraordinary will heaven and its surroundings be.

The Islamic Life

An Islamic life comes into being like a tree. A verdant tree can only grow when it has learned to blend with the terrestrial and celestial orders of nature; likewise a person becomes Islamic by deriving spiritual nourishment from the whole of God's universe.

Ritual practices and revolutionary slogans do not

go to make an Islamic life. One can only become a true Muslim when one begins to receive the light of God. God has provided a world of nourishment for trees; in like manner, spiritual nourishment is always available to man. Just as the mighty oak springs from the acorn buried deep in the womb of nature, so an Islamic life grows from deeply-rooted faith. Be it man or tree, both have to attach themselves to vaster orders if they are to reach perfection. The difference is that trees come into existence involuntarily, whereas man can only develop of his own free will.

Those who thrive on God's spiritual provision in this world will flourish in the hereafter. Those who neglected to partake of such provision will be raised from the dead in a spiritually impoverished state, no matter how splendid was their condition on earth.

The Believer: God's Industry

Everyone is an industry. Some produce nothing but flames and poison in the sense that they make arrogant misuse of their power whenever they are given the opportunity; they are ostentatious in their expenditure; they aim at the destruction of those who are under their command; they are bitter and malignant towards those with whom they disagree; they are selfish, unjust and stubborn in their dealings.

Such people have established an infernal industry within themselves. Whatever enters into them comes out in an evil form. They will find themselves engulfed by that which they have produced. They will enter a fire of their own making.

Others respond to the possession of power in a humble manner. They are quick to acknowledge just criticism. They spend their wealth for the cause of God. They do not assert themselves when given the opportunity; they prefer to adopt an attitude of humility and attribute all credit to God alone. They are just and benevolent towards those who are at their mercy.

Such people have established God's industry within themselves. Whatever enters into them is moulded into a divine form. They are cultivating a crop of fragrant flowers in this world, and they will abide eternally in the gardens which they have cultivated on earth.

Action or Acknowledgement

True faith should become an integral part of one's thinking. It should permeate one's heart and mind. Everything — one's thoughts and desires, one's love and fear should be subordinated to one's faith. This is the supreme degree of faith. One who is of such faith is protected by God in this world, and one who is provided with divine protection on earth is sure of it in the hereafter.

There are other believers who do both good and evil, but they admit their faults. Hopefully, God will forgive them, for He is forgiving and merciful.

The strong in faith act according to their belief, but those who are weaker in their faith cannot achieve such consistency in thought, word and deed. They, too, will receive God's eternal blessings, but to do so, they should show contrition and not persist in their errors; they should openly admit their faults and not try to justify them; they should confess their guilt instead of trying to explain it away; they should show no signs of irritation when their faults are pointed out, but should bow in acquiescence; they should make up, with tears of humble entreaty, for what they lack in virtue. Those who do not even have this much to offer cannot expect forgiveness from God.

The Long Road of Patience

God's beloved servant strives to please God, not himself; he follows the path of truth rather than the dictates of his own self; he attaches more importance to honour in the next life than to worldly prestige; he does not revenge himself on others, even if they wrong him time and time again. This is the path of patience. Certainly, the road of patience is long and arduous, but it is the only road that can lead one to paradise. Paradise will be granted to the patient, and the patient are those who are willing to bear every loss for God's sake.

In this world of trial, one is bound to encounter difficulties and setbacks. Those who desire paradise should know that the path that they will have to tread will not be an easy one: they will have to bear with persecution from others; they will have to endure protracted periods of waiting; they will have to put up with persecution from rivals. Those who are seeking the truth should be careful not to lose patience and succumb to stresses and strains. If they do, they will lose their way to paradise, and will not be able to reach their destination.

The road to paradise is one long road of patience. Only those who are willing to bear the hardships of patience, who carry on regardless of every hurt, who turn the other cheek to every blow, will be worthy to enter heaven.

God's Tree

A tree is but a manifestation of a seed's potential to derive sustenance from earth and water, and produce one of the most beautiful sights in the world in the form of a trunk, branches, leaves and flowers.

Man is much the same as a tree. He has been put on earth like a seed. But he can only grow into a tree by virtue of his own efforts. Providence, however, has granted him innumerable sources of nourishment, and opportunities exist on earth for man to build an eternal future for himself. His efforts on earth will have the reward of the verdant gardens of paradise in the next world. He will dwell there in eternal contentment.

But those who do not partake of this divine sustenance are like seeds which are cast on to a rock or on barren land. Such seeds will never grow into trees. One who does not make use of the opportunities for growth in this world is like a defective seed which never grows into a tree. Such a person will meet with eternal failure. The world which he will inherit in the next life will be a total desert.

A heavenly soul is like a fine tree which grows in this world and is then transplanted in God's evergreen garden in the after-life.

The Inheritance of Paradise

The freedom which man has been given on earth is not permanent. It has been granted to him for a certain time and for a specific reason: that he may be put to the test. God wishes to see who make good use of their freedom, so that He may reward such people. Those who are spoiled by their freedom will be cast into Hell.

The world will end when the test of man is complete. When man's test has run its course, the Lord will take over direct control of the earth, as He has already done with the rest of the universe. Then the good will be separated from the bad. The good will inherit life everlasting in heaven, while the wicked will be condemned to eternal punishment.

Those who are worthy of abiding in the future world of heaven are being selected in this world. Those who obey God, despite their freedom, and voluntarily impose the will of God upon themselves, are deserving of paradise. During the period of man's trial, all kinds of people have been allowed to inhabit the world. When the trial of man has run its course, however, only the righteous will be fit to inherit the evergreen world of God. Others will be denied entrance into heaven; they will be cast into a world of everlasting anguish and despair.

Selection for Paradise

Man has been granted freedom in this world of trial and tribulation, but he has misused his freedom and has sown cruelty and corruption on earth. How can God tolerate so much evil? The only possible answer is that, without it, those noble souls who are fit to abide in paradise would not stand out from the others. There would be no basis on which to select them. Only if man is free can he prove that he is willing to renounce all power for God's sake alone. The unbounded evil which exists on earth is, in fact, the price that has to be paid for unbounded good. On the strength of this good, a selection is made on earth, from the mass of humanity, of those blessed souls who, consciously and of their own free will, are obedient to God; who submit to the Lord on principle, and not because they are forced to do so.

Such people stand head and shoulders above the rest of mankind. They could deny the truth, but they do not do so. They could give precedence to themselves, but they always put God first. They could establish themselves in seats of power, but they waive all claims to power and follow truth and justice. Man has to be free to prove himself fit for paradise; he must also pay the price for his freedom.

Two Kinds of Soul

There are two types of human beings: those who follow base desires and those who adopt a pure way of life. There are those who despise others and thrive on ostentatious and self-centered pursuits. Their souls are inimical to truth and their minds are full of selfish and conceited thoughts. They like inconveniencing others; they derive immense pleasure from taking advantage of the weaknesses of others. Such people are living on infernal provision, and will abide in Hell in the Hereafter.

Then there are those who are pure in spirit. Others' success causes them genuine pleasure. They are happy to forgive those who are at their mercy. They are loving and wish their fellows well; they thrive on humility and meekness. Such people are living in a heavenly atmosphere. They are content to concede a disputed point to others. When their faults are pointed out they are quick to admit them. They are restless until they have paid back their debts. Such people are living on heavenly provision; they will abide eternally in the lush gardens of paradise.

Thankfulness

Man is never satisfied with what he has; he always seeks more. As a result, he never ceases to be discontented. God has favoured everyone in some way or another, but man is more concerned with what he does not have; he pays scant regard to what he has. People who have this attitude cannot be moved to offer thanks to God. They are lacking in that priceless virtue which is essential for admission into paradise.

No one can be absolutely happy on earth. That is the way the world has been made. If cold climates have their drawbacks, so do hot climates. If low-income groups encounter difficulties, so do high-income groups. If the weak have a hard life, neither is it easy for those who wield power. There is no end to the problems of this world, but man should persevere in spite of all the difficulties he encounters, for he is being tested in this world. He should concentrate on earning God's pleasure, and not on achieving a trouble-free life, for that is something which can only be achieved in the next world.

The greatest offering that anyone who wishes to earn a place in paradise can offer his Lord is a thankful heart. The only way to cultivate a feeling of thankfulness is to rise above the difficulties and problems of life. The price of heaven is gratitude; only those who have paid this price will enter heaven.

Godly People

Most people seem to be devoted to God under normal conditions. Then, when something untoward happens, they suddenly change. Emotions like love and hate, questions of honour and prestige overcome them and push their attachment to God into the background. They are devout under normal conditions, but in extraordinary situations, they act like people who have no thought of God.

Those who are really devoted to God fear Him at all times. They do not let themselves be led astray by their love for someone; they stay within the bounds that God has laid down. They are never overcome by hate; they are just with everyone, even with their enemies. Worldly honour and prestige can never prevent them from acknowledging the truth.

God's true servants earnestly seek to rectify themselves; they are conscious of their faults; they constantly scrutinize their actions and are able to see themselves objectively; they look at themselves from a realistic point of view—the point of view from which God looks at them.

These are the ones who will be admitted into God's paradise. There they will know neither affliction nor fear.

The Seeker Finds

People take heaven's name but act in a manner more fitting for Hell. This means that they have never sought heaven from God; if they had, God would never have let them proceed on a path which can only lead them to Hell.

It is impossible that one should ask God for heaven and be given hell instead; that one should seek to fear the Lord and that He should harden one's heart; that one should desire to remember the Lord at all times and that He should leave one in a state of forgetfulness; that one should long to aspire to eternity and that God should fill one's heart with love of the world: that one should aspire to true, heartfelt piety and that He should make one's piety spiritless; that one should wish to worship God and that he should let one worship personalities instead.

If one does not have what is desirable in life, it means that one has not sought it. Those who seek will always find. How can the Lord of Universe leave His servant in such a state that he will be able to cry out on the Day of Resurrection, "Lord, I asked You for heaven and You have given me Hell." Truly, this is out of the question. One cannot conceive of such a thing happening. There is not a day on which the Lord does not grant His mercy to His servants; yet He gives only to those who ask. One cannot blame the Bestower if the recipient has no desire for what He has to offer.

Citizen of Paradise

In heaven God's praises will be sung on all sides; only He will be glorified. Only those who praise and glorify God on earth will be fit to enter such a heaven. If one attributes greatness to oneself or other people, then how can one be fit for heaven? Words will accord with actions in paradise. There will be no deceit there. People will not exploit others, or hurt others' feelings. Only those who have proved by their actions on earth that they are capable of living up to such high standards will be admitted into paradise.

Heaven will be a world full of positive actions. Only those who think positively on earth will be able to enter such a heaven. Those who engage in negative and destructive pursuits in this world cannot hope to enter paradise in the next world. Man will not be able to hurt man in heaven. Only those who have no. harboured jealous or evil thoughts towards others will be deserving of such a paradise, for only by refraining from harming others can one show that one is worthy of being preserved from evil oneself. Heaven will be free of impurity and frivolity. Only those who refrain from vain and base pursuits in this world will be granted entry into this heavenly abode.

Submission to God

Man can come close to God only through humility. God's favour falls upon those of his servants who are humble. If humility is not forced, but comes from the heart, it will be more precious to one than anything else. Real humility is to acknowledge one's true position on earth. Humility brings one close to God.

A person who does not know what it is to be humble cannot derive pleasure from his worship. If one's life is based on discrimination, one cannot appreciate the equality of man. An egocentric person cannot taste the joy of recognizing God's greatness. Those who delight in proving others wrong cannot realize the delight of discovering and admitting their own errors. Those who are used to applying one set of values to themselves and a different set to others cannot understand that judging oneself by the same standards as one sets for others is the greatest wealth in life.

Heaven is for those who delight in heavenly actions; whose worship and whole way of life take on a heavenly hue. A heavenly person will restrain jealous feelings and suppress the urge for vengeance. He will rise above sectarian prejudices. He will act fairly towards everyone—even those he disagrees with. He will judge people on the grounds of truth; he will not be influenced by false pretensions. Only he who is so enamoured of such conduct that he cannot depart from it under any circumstances is truly fit for paradise.

The Lesson of a Tree

Take a look at a tree. Its trunk is firm and solid, but its leaves, fruits and flowers are weak and impermanent. Yet the beauty of its leaves, the colourfulness of its flowers, and the delicacy of its fruits show that these less substantial parts of the tree have deserved greater attention from nature than the stronger parts. It seems as if the trunk and the branches were created to bring into existence the fragile masterpieces of creation called leaves, flowers and fruits.

This is a sign of God, showing man what his Lord requires of him, and what he should do to make the tree of his life blossom. A tree shows man that he should seek the meaning of things beneath the surface; he should not be over-impressed by outward strength. People who adopt this attitude to life will be admitted into paradise.

Those who will not be admitted include the man who worships stone and ignores truth; who is polite and humane towards the mighty, and looks down with disdain on those towards whom God would really like him to be polite and humane. He is charitable for the sake of fame and withholds charity when there is no fame to be gained, though that is the only charity acceptable to God.

Belonging to the next World

Heaven belongs to those who long for it. To one who really longs for heaven, everything else seems insignificant in comparison. Things of the world lose their value. Eternal matters become so important in his sight that worldly matters pale into insignificance.

When does one really belong to the next world? When one is so absorbed in thoughts of the hereafter that one tends to forget worldly matters. When one is so concerned with eternity that one forgets earthly concerns. When one is so preoccupied with thoughts of eternal content and torment that one's position in the world ceases to seem important. When one is so drawn towards life everlasting that one seems to be neglectful of the present world. When one's concentration is so fixed on sublime realities that one lives in this world, but is not of it. When the sight of worldly luxury only makes one wonder what will befall one in eternity. When affliction makes one cry out, "Lord, I cannot bear worldly torment; how will I be able to withstand the torments of the next world." When one neither derives satisfaction from the pleasures of this world, nor is affected by worldly difficulties.

Only when all of these conditions are fulfilled can one truly be said to have faith in the life to come. The gates to heaven will be opened for such fortunate souls.

❧

Heavenly Conduct

Heavenly conduct has repercussions within a human being; it brings the verdure of paradise to the soul. One might seem to be active, but if one is not benefiting spiritually from one's actions, then they are worthless. Truly virtuous action should spark off divine consciousness in one's mind; it should make one's heart beat with a divine rhythm; it should move one's soul to ecstasy; it should make something tremendous happen within one, to open a window on sublime realities.

What is important as far as the next life is concerned is not what one is doing, but what one is becoming. One may be very busy in life; one may have a long list of achievements to one's credit; but if one is inwardly unaffected, then one's actions are futile. What is the good of the wind if it does not carry oxygen? What is the good of water if it does not quench one's thirst? What is the good of food if it fails to nourish? What is the good of the sun if it does not produce light? If all these things were present without their properties, then they might as well not be there at all.

One who is not fit for heaven utters empty words which do not echo within him. He acts, but his actions do not touch his soul. On the contrary, the actions of a godly person are spiritual experience in themselves; they provide nourishment for his soul. His external actions deeply stir his innermost being.

Who will be Granted Paradise?

Paradise cannot be gained at a paltry price; it belongs only to those fortunate souls who prove themselves to be God's true servants. Belief does not just mean adding some rituals to a normal worldly life; true belief entails the governance of one's whole life by Islam; it means devoting oneself heart and soul to the worship of God.

Islam should radically change a person's life, for the believer finds God so close that he enters into communion with Him. Angels become his companions in times of solitude. He keeps his tongue in check, being conscious of his responsibilities to the Lord. He strictly obeys God's commandments. True Islam makes a person live in this world as if he were standing before God and being judged.

The awareness of truth which comes to believers in this world will come to unbelievers only after death, when it is too late. When God becomes visible to man, all will believe in Him, but the believer has faith while God is still invisible. True believers anticipate the severity of the Day of Resurrection in the world: others will have that experience only in the next world.

Who will be Saved

To be deserving of heaven in the next world, one must experience it in this world: one must attain the spiritual uplift which will qualify one for heaven in the hereafter. Fear of Judgement Day should make the hair on one's body stand on end. One's heart should be illuminated by manifestations of God's glory, which make one feel close to Him. One should suppress feelings of anger and vengeance, demonstrating thus what the forgiveness of the Lord will be like. One should witness through one's own tears of contrition the scene of a forgiving master pardoning his repentant servant. One should pardon those who are at one's mercy, in the hope that God will be forgiving on the day that one will be totally at His mercy. One should control one's tongue, though one is able to speak at will. One should bow before the truth on earth, as others will in eternity.

The believer is a flower of the garden of paradise, which sprouts in this world and blossoms in the next. He experiences in this world what others will experience after death, when it is too late. People's reaction to the various circumstances they face in life will determine whether they are fit for heaven or Hell; if they respond in a satanic manner they, prove themselves fit for Hell, and if they respond in an angelic manner, they prove themselves worthy of heaven.

Without Paying the Price

Man has to offer his own being in return for paradise. Whoever sacrifices his life for God will find eternal reward. There is no other way of earning salvation.

There comes a time in everybody's life when one has to sacrifice something—one's self, one's honour, one's property or one's life itself—for the sake of one's religion. Whoever makes the required sacrifices at such times is worthy of God's favour. Whoever stops short of self-sacrifices in God's path will be permanently denied His blessings.

Paradise is so priceless that nothing we have can pay for it. God has nonetheless put a trivial price on it, that is, the sacrifice that we must make for it. The only thing that lies between man and paradise is that he should give up his insignificant self to God; that he should expend all his paltry wealth for the sake of God; that he should spend his time on earth serving God. To accept truth is a sacrifice; to give up one's wealth for the cause of God is a sacrifice; to spend one's time and energy working for God's cause is a sacrifice; to put up with displeasing circumstances for God's sake is a sacrifice.

What a small price to have to pay for such a great

gift! Yet man is so unwilling to pay even this paltry price, that he passes his short time on earth without doing so.

Heavenly Actions

Those who delight in heavenly action in this world will taste the delights of paradise in eternity. Heaven is for those who depend more on God's invisible support than on the visible props of this world; who love and fear God above all things; who are willing to obey the Prophet under any circumstances; to whom eternity matters more than this world; who prefer to acknowledge truth than to reject it; who derive more satisfaction from tears shed for God's sake than from heedless peals of laughter. If a question of pride comes in the way of acknowledging the truth, they are ready to accept the truth at the cost of wounded pride. Forgiving those who wrong them pleases them more than seeking revenge. Fairness to others' is dearer to them than usurpation of others' rights. They prefer to suppress the feelings of envy and contempt which flare up within them than to express them. They do not form a bad opinion of others, but prefer to think well of everyone.

The Heavenly Traveller

God requires man to offer up his wealth for God's sake. In return, He has promised man salvation in the next world.

Man evades his responsibilities, excusing himself on the grounds of the difficulties of life, but these difficulties are precious opportunities which could be availed of to please his Lord. The stumbling blocks which hinder a person in real submission to God are, in fact, openings for spiritual enlightenment. They provide him with opportunities for real progress. Life's tribulations should not discourage one: one should overcome them and continue on one's journey, for they are stages on the path to God.

God's most beloved servant is the one who suppresses his desires for God's sake; who gives up the comforts of life on His behalf; who surmounts all obstacles in his journey towards God. One does not succeed in this world by accumulating wealth; one succeeds by spending one's wealth in the cause of God.

The healthiest are those who have lost their health in the path of God. The richest are those who have impoverished themselves for God's sake. The highest in esteem are those who have lost worldly esteem in the service of the Lord. The most fortunate are those who reach their Lord with nothing but good deeds to their credit. These are the ones on whom God will shower His mercy.

The Inheritance of Paradise

The believer is like a solid tree, which is nourished by the whole universe. Sustained by his belief, he grows like a splendid tree, with his roots spread out under the ground and his branches reaching up into the sky. Never deserted by divine succour, he exudes freshness and vitality at all times. He prospers in this world and the next.

The unbeliever, on the other hand, is like a bramble bush, or a weed which grows on the surface of the earth, bereft of divine succour. He is unstable in this world, and will give no fruit in the next. He loses out in both places.

God has given unbelievers some rein in this ephemeral world, and the opportunities they have been given on earth should be seen in this light. Since they are being tested in this world, they have the chance to grow and develop temporarily on earth. But when the period of trial has run its course, they will burn forever. The only souls to inherit the luxuriant world of paradise will be those who have shown a true devotion to the Lord on earth.

Heavenly Character

God requires men of excellence to take up their abode in paradise. To this end, He has provided models throughout the cosmos to inspire human beings to attain that level of excellence. Take the iron found in the cosmos. That is man's model for human resoluteness. The water which gushes forth from barren rocks is his model for leniency and compassion. The immutability of the laws of nature shows man how faithfully he must keep his promises. The fragrance, colour and beauty of the material world are there to inspire man to deal equitably with others. The fact that billions of stars remain in orbit without colliding is an example of how man should operate within his own sphere and avoid clashing with others. Returning good for evil is exemplified by the trees who take in harmful carbon dioxide and supply us with life-giving oxygen in return. The mountains and everything that stands erect cast their shadows on the ground as if in self-prostration: man is required in the same way to be humble. He should never be proud or domineering. Whoever wishes to share in God's eternal blessings should be pleased only with that which pleases God; he should obey God, as the cosmos does.

The iron of the cosmos should be the model for human resoluteness. The water which flows forth from

189

hard rocks gives man the example of leniency and compassion. The laws of nature are immutable; so man is required to be faithful to his promises. The world of matter is fragrant, colourful and elegant; man following the same pattern should deal equitably with others. Billions of stars revolve continuously, but never collide with one another; man following this cosmic pattern should operate within his own sphere, being careful to avoid clashing with others. Trees take in carbon dioxide and supply us with oxygen in return; this action is required on a human level in the observance of certain ethical values, such as doing good to those who harm one. Mountains, and everything that stands erect, cast their shadows on the ground as if in an act of self-prostration; so man is required to be humble in the same way; he should not be domineering or proud.

People of Paradise

Those who live by the Book of God receive God's special favours in this world, and are promised heaven in the next world. But they will be granted them solely on the basis of their own actions. People of the Book tend to forget this proviso: they take it for granted that, whether they follow God's commandments or not, God's promise to them will be fulfilled, and they will surely enter the kingdom of heaven.

True religious spirit makes one realistic. As long as the followers of revealed religions possess this spirit, they will realize that God is just, and will reward people according to their actions alone.

On the other hand, when people lose the true religious spirit, they take to wishful thinking. Real actions give way to false hopes. They think that they will be admitted into paradise because they belong to a certain community, whether they do good deeds or not.

Success in the hereafter is for those who conform to divine justice on earth; who live according to the will of God; who fear Hell before confronting it, and long for heaven before seeing it.

৯৯

Eternal Bliss

God's acceptance of righteous actions is marked by wondrous sensations which introduce one to the heaven which has been promised to God's true servants in the life to come. Thus believers discover the fragrance of the garden of paradise in this world. They hold such sensations dearer than all worldly pleasures.

When one gives true charity to a needy person and finds the rewards with God: when the recitation of the

Qur'an brings tears into one's eyes: when one experiences moments of anguish which make one feel close to God; when one's voice trembles and one's heart throbs as one utters the prayers which God has put into one's heart; then one is partaking of the provision of the Lord in spiritual form. One is tasting of the fruits of paradise, which God has kept in store for his righteous servants.

The thrills of true faith are the form which the fruits of paradise take in this world. In eternity they will take the form of the everlasting blessings of heaven.

If one is not close to God in this world, then how can one hope to be close to Him in the next world? If one does not derive joy from one's worship in this world, then how can one hope to be rewarded with eternal bliss in the hereafter?

A Flower of Paradise

The true believer is a flower of paradise. His fragrance is manifested in the form of divine characteristics in this life, which will be transformed into tangible blessings in the hereafter. Heaven is another name for these blessings.

The believer is one who is so involved in the hereafter that he becomes indifferent to the world. He puts up with any sufferings that others may cause him. He is so conscious of his own failures that he does not mind being criticized. If others humiliate him, he forgives them for God's sake. His heart has been purified by true devotion to God, so he forgives and forgets others' excesses. He is so free of malice that he prays for those who wrong him.

God is pleased with such souls and will admit them into paradise. Paradise is a refined world which only refined souls can enter. Those who lead negative lives and act in a spiteful manner are not worthy to dwell in it.

People think that they are bound for heaven, but they are far adrift from that destination.

Those Who Bow Before God

God requires for paradise realistic souls who live as if they are seeing God, though He is invisible; who are so conscious of God's greatness and perfection that He is always in their thoughts. Their lives should be so centred on God that their hearts should pulsate to His words.

The wondrous world of paradise will be inhabited by those who are so devoted to God that He comes to dominate their lives; who raise their consciousness to a level which enables them to look at themselves objectively; who, although they are free, place constraints upon themselves and practise self-discipline.

When one reaches this stage of high-mindedness and realism, one develops objectivity in one's thinking; one begins to see oneself in a true rather than a personal light; one submits totally to the Creator, though one is not forced to do so; one keeps to God's commandments, even in the face of temptation; one accepts truth fully, even though one is in a position to reject it; one has the same attitude of submission to the Lord of Creation now, when He is invisible, as one will have when He becomes visible in the hereafter.

Virtuous Life

Those who are patient and do not despair in the face of disaster, are fit to live in paradise. They pray for those who hurt them. They do not mind being criticised. They act justly to everyone, even those who wrong them. They are fair and honest in their dealings with others.

The true believer requites evil with good. Only those who are ever mindful of God are blessed with pure lives of this nature, that is, those who discover

God on such a profound level that He permeates their beings and becomes the focal point of their emotions.

Where unbelievers are arrogant, believers bow in humility. Where unbelievers are contemptuous, believers are considerate. Where unbelievers bear ill-will, believers are well-wishing. Where unbelievers usurp others' right, believers render to everyone his due. Believers are not prevented by false pride from acknowledging the truth. Believers never forsake justice, even when they are tempted to seek revenge.

God's Envoy

Those who are bathed in the light of God are fit to preach the word of God. Whatever they say comes from Him. Thus it becomes possible for them to sing God's eternal praises on earth. Yet man does not take heed. His heart remains sealed.

Preaching God's word is not like playing a record. One can only preach when one has experienced something like a volcanic eruption within one's soul. A preacher's whole being must be deeply involved in what he says and writes. His song is not just words and music; it is an expression of a delicate spiritual communion with the Lord.

But how strange it is that even such divine words

fail to move people's hearts. The preacher warns his people with earnestness and intensity, and his whole being testifies to the truth of this warning, but people are deaf to his call. He pipes to his people but they do not lament. He shows people the kingdom of heaven, but they are not enraptured. He warns them of a blazing Hell, but they show no fear. He explains to people the signs of God, but they do not fall prostrate.

Man proves himself to be the most insensitive, although allegedly the most sensitive of all God's creatures.

PART FIVE

The Fire of Hell

The Reality of Life

There is only one God. He has created all things. All men will return to Him after death, and He will judge them according to their actions on earth. Some will be rewarded with eternal paradise, while others will be condemned to hellfire. Everyone shall meet the fate he merits, be he weak or strong.

When one realizes this grave reality, one's life changes completely. One becomes careful to avoid that which will lead one to Hell, and desirous of anything which will make one deserving of paradise. One comes to love and fear God above all else.

When one fears God and is conscious of one's eternal destiny, one becomes extremely cautious in one's dealings with one's fellow men. By mistreating others, one feels as if one is exposing oneself to the fire of hell. One is never arrogant, for one realizes that it is not just humans one is dealing with; every man is supported by the power of God and His angels. One is never unjust when dealing with one's fellow, for one knows that eventually one is going to have to answer before God for one's actions. One does not see others as mere people; one realizes that Almighty God is also standing by their side. What we must do is strive to save ourselves and our fellows from the punishment of the next world. The prophets have taught that man should make every effort to save himself from eternal doom. We must do our utmost to protect ourselves from the torment of Judgement Day and exhort others to do the same. There is no task in life more important than this. This is the Muslims' fundamental task. Only if they perform this task can they hope to obtain that which they desire in this world.

Inner Revolution

God is the greatest of all powers. No one can escape His reckoning. He will deal severely with the wicked. Belief in a God of this awesome nature is no simple matter; faith transforms a person's being when it enters his soul.

Imagine the change that comes over a person who suddenly realizes that a lion is roaming free in front of him. A far greater change occurs when one truly realizes the existence of God. To believe in God is to discover Him, and when one truly discovers God, one becomes more certain of His existence than of anything else; one fears Him above all else.

Faith in God is like an earthquake which shakes the human soul. The true believer sees the Day of

Resurrection before it comes.

Such belief engulfs one's entire being in the fear of God. This fear is manifested in all one's dealings with others. One does not humiliate the weak, for one sees that they are God's envoys. One does not cower before the strong, because one sees that all are helpless before God. One accepts the truth when it is proven, for denying it would be like seeing heaven and Hell before one, then leaving the fresh gardens of paradise to plunge into the flames of Hell.

The Trial of Man

When one considers one's dealings with others in purely human terms, one is apt to resort to cruelty and injustice. If one were to be aware of the presence of God, one would be careful to avoid all injustice and cruelty.

All worldly events occur by God's leave. Everything fits in with a divine scheme according to which man is tested by the Lord. Everything happens so that those concerned may be tested. A person's calibre can only be made out from the way he responds to life's situations.

In all worldly matters we are being tested as to whether we are just in our treatment of one another.

We are being tested, in the various situations we have to deal with in life, as to whether we are consistent in the values we apply, or whether we have one set of values for ourselves and another set for others. In the decisions we have to take in life, we are being tested as to whether we follow a policy of convenience, or stick to what is right.

Our future fate is being decided on the basis of our present performance. We can either make use of our opportunities on earth to deserve a place for ourselves in paradise, or we can waste them and condemn ourselves to punishment in Hell.

What Man should Realize

Man thinks he is free to do and say what he likes in this world. He accumulates wealth and thinks it will ensure his future security. He wields power fearlessly, certain that it will never be taken away from him. People are sure of themselves in this world. They have no idea of the fate that is in store for them. Eventually death will put paid to the false security they feel in this world. They will be transported in a helpless state with dreadful suddenness to the next world.

No one can escape this fate. When death comes, we will realize, with terror in our hearts, how wrong we had been about things in this world. What seems real to us in this world is, in fact, only a deception; the reality of things will only be revealed to us after death.

A person's attitudes will suddenly change when he perceives reality. "Lord," he will cry, "I thought I was free in the world, but my freedom was only an illusion. I thought I was rich, but I have turned out to be destitute. I considered myself powerful, but now I have been exposed for the helpless creature that I was. I thought I had many friends in the world, but they have all deserted me; there is no one to help me now."

This is what man should realize. But unfortunately man has forgotten that this is the reality that is going to affect him more than anything.

Doomsday

People eat, drink and make merry in this world. They establish themselves in comfortable homes. They seek to win promotion in life. They believe or reject matters at will. They are free to do and say what they like. They strive to excel in whatever department of life they choose.

Man has been deluded by his worldly position. He thinks that what he owns in this world will always be his. He forgets that he is being put to the test by means of all the power which he wields in this ephemeral world. Nothing that he has will last. Everything will be taken away from him. He will be stripped of even the most basic of the worldly amenities he used to enjoy. He will be brought before the Lord of the Universe to be judged.

All disparity between men will disappear on the Day of Judgement. Fear of God will seal everybody's tongue. Injustice will benefit no one; truth will be inescapable. Man will stand alone, answerable for his actions.

We must foresee the coming of that day before its arrival. Those who fail to see it coming before it is upon them will have to pay dearly for their shortsightedness. They will have to endure the punishment of hell-fire.

Credit Alone

Man has no intrinsic power. No one can, by himself, give anything to, or take anything away from anyone. All events happen by the will of God. Man exists in this world to be tested, and the test of man concerns his intentions alone, for man can only wish for an event to take place; he cannot actually make things happen.

Everything that happens in this world seems to have a cause, but these 'causes' are no more than a veil over reality. Cause and effect are beyond the powers of man.

These tasks are accomplished by God through His angels.

Man is being tested in this world by means of the situations with which God confronts him from day to day. God wishes to see how he reacts to these situations. Sometimes he is being tested as to whether he upholds the cause of truth, or forsakes the truth and follows a false path. Sometimes he is being tested as to whether he is just in his treatment of others or not. Sometimes he is being tested as to whether he is true to his word, or breaks promises after they are made.

All worldly events occur by the will of God. Man simply takes credit for what happens, whether good or bad.

Seeing into the Future

In order to put man to the test in this world, God has given him some power. Everybody has been granted a certain domain in which he is able to act at will. Some have more scope to act than others, but everyone acts, within his own domain, as others act in theirs. It makes no difference whether the power one wields is minimal or great. Everyone misuses it in much the same way. Different as people may seem, in reality they are all the same.

People, seeking to prove themselves, are always trying to further their own interests at the expense of others. They overestimate their power and consider that they can usurp others in order to establish themselves. They do not realize that it is not anyone's vacant seat that awaits them: it is their own graves. Those who seek to destroy others are bound to be destroyed themselves. Those who would like to see others dead and buried are soon to suffer that very fate themselves.

Those who consider themselves successful today will have to face failure in the future. We are being reminded of this daily, but no one takes heed. Everyone is too engrossed in the present. No one cares to look beyond the present into the future.

Those who are caught up in the present should begin to look into the future, for the present will soon pass, it is in the future that the day of reckoning lies. We shall then have to face the consequences of that day for all time to come.

✿

Before Time Runs Out

Man is on trial in this world. Here, everyone is being tested: if one acts rightly, one will succeed in the trial of life. Neglect of the task that lies before one is tantamount to failure. Those who do not strive to succeed in the trial of life are doomed to failure, whether they like it or not.

Man can be likened to an ice-vendor in this respect, one whose ice is continually melting and who has to sell his merchandise before it all dissolves. If he delays in selling the ice, then he will have nothing left to sell; his capital and his profits will have vanished into thin air.

This same principle applies to the life of man. Man is rapidly moving towards a sorry end. There is only one thing he can do to avoid disaster, and that is to put the time he has been allotted on earth to the best possible use.

A successful ice-vendor is one who sells his ice before it has all dissolved. Similarly a successful person is one who puts his life to good use before it ends, and prepares for the life to come before it is upon him.

ৡ

When Will They Ever Learn?

Man has been given freedom of choice in this world, for this world is for the trial of man, and man can only be tested if he is free to do as he wills— if he is free to choose between right and wrong, and free to use the opportunities and potentialities which he has been given in whatever manner he chooses. His freedom, however, will be short-lived.

If anyone wishes to reject the truth in this world,

he will have no difficulty in finding words with which to justify himself. If anyone wishes to deny the true call to religion, he will find other beliefs in which he can take refuge. If anyone chooses to ignore God's call, he will find other things to hold on to in this world which will lull him into a false sense of security. When the true nature of things is revealed, however, the props on which he depended in the world will be exposed as false and unreal.

When man rises from the dead, and God appears in all His glory, man will be helpless before the Lord. He will have no choice but to accept that which he used to deny in the world.

If man only knew the awesome nature of the last day, he would cease the vain conversations in which he endlessly indulges in this world; he would refrain from all the crimes which no humanitarian or moral exhortation could prevent him from committing.

The Tragedy of Man

Man has lost all sense of reality in this world. So lost has he become in his own vainglory that he has forgotten the greater glory of God. Although man is constantly being reminded of his helplessness, before death he thinks he has power; in fact, he is nothing but a pawn of the reality which he chooses to ignore.

Man breaks his promises; he does not pay people their due; he does not bow to the truth; he accuses others, but fails to admit his own mistakes; he turns away from the weak and hails the strong; he bases his life on desire rather than on principle; he persecutes the downtrodden and cowers before the mighty; he concentrates on himself rather than on God. Fear of Hell and desire for heaven do not dominate his life; he is guided by worldly apprehensions and desires alone. Man continues in his evil ways and forgets that in so doing he is moving further away from Paradise and drawing closer to Hell. This is the tragedy of man; he does not care for that which is most to be desired; he does not fear that which is most to be feared.

No Refuge

One who does not bow before the truth but cringes before worldly might, who is not persuaded by sound reasoning but cowers in submission when there is any threat of force, is worthy of going to Hell.

Whereas in eternity God Himself will appear directly before men, in this world there can only be indirect evidence of His existence. To bow before the evidence of God is to bow before God Himself. Those who do so will be admitted into Paradise. Those who do not bow before the evidence of God in this world have, in effect, refused to bow before God Himself. They will be punished for their rebelliousness and will be consigned to Hell.

When the truth is proclaimed by some insignificant person, those who deny it are sure that they cannot be harmed. They forget that it is not some weak person's word they are denying; it is the word of God. Their action amounts to a rejection of God Himself and the whole universe rejects one who rejects God. They will be left to wander aimlessly, with no refuge in heaven or on earth.

The day is coming when those who rely on false evidence will have to face the truth, when those who are settled in the world will be rendered homeless and those who are secure will not find a blade of grass on which to stand.

Wishful Thinking

People seek their own happiness in other's pain. They oppress those who are close to them and attempt to make a name for themselves amongst the far-distant. They are unjust in their private lives, but put on a show of justice in public. They cannot bear to hear themselves criticized, but consider themselves as having been appointed by God to criticise others. They are expert in detecting the faults of others, while ignoring their own.

But the reward of God will be reserved for those who give others what is due to them, and who do no wrong to their neighbours; who are not selfish in their dealings with others, but think in terms of what is fair and just; who do not think of their own interest when the truth is at stake; who lose themselves in the greatness of God.

People are playing with fire, but have no idea of the consequences of their deeds. They are careering towards Hell but are happy in the mistaken idea that they are well on the way to heaven. One can but pity those who have only false hopes to their credit, and who seek to make capital out of such wishful thinking. One can only pity those who want to fashion, in the world created by God, a world of their own choice—which is not permissible in the eyes of the Almighty.

Angelic or Satanic

God's faithful servants act on angelic promptings, while the rebellious take their cue from the devil. The source of people's guidance is clear from their actions and speech.

Those who live in the company of angels are humble in times of disagreement and quick to bow to the truth. They show by their actions that they have been guided on to the path of the angels, for angels are never proud; they show no hesitation in bowing to the truth.

The devil's way is very different. Those who follow it are cruel and vindictive in times of disagreement. They are haughty in their dealings with others. They are following in the devil's footsteps. Arrogance and self-assertiveness are attributes of the devil: the Quran has made this clear.

Ignorance of death and of the resurrection of man gives people the courage to indulge in injustice and contumacy in this world. If people knew what was coming to them they would stop dead, in fear; their tongues would freeze into silence. They would not try to justify their mistakes; they would immediately admit that they were wrong.

When God Appears

When one truly discovers God, one realizes that He cannot have created man and the rest of the world in vain. God has created the universe: He sustains it in its functioning. How can an almighty and all-knowing God such as He let the whole cosmic machine grind on pointlessly without its meaning ever being revealed?

Faith does more than this for a person. It instills in one the firm conviction that God will Himself eventually appear before man. In this world He remains hidden, though His presence is felt as He guides and sustains the universe. Faith tells one that the manifestation of the Lord will be an event of the greatest relevance. God is both mighty and just; He is aware of all things; His appearance will bring justice to the world. When God comes before mankind, those who refused to serve Him on earth will be brought low before Him. They will appear more despicable than insects. On the other hand, those faithful servants of God, who devoted themselves entirely to Him, will be honoured in heaven.

God's invisibility in the world seemingly gives unbelievers the licence to run amok. But when God appears before mankind, only the faithful will be honoured. They will inherit a new, complete and everlasting world in which they will enjoy the eternal delights of paradise, while those who defied God in the world will be thrown into the fire of Hell.

The Lesson of Death

Man desires life, but, sooner or later, he has to come to terms with death. Just as he is at the peak of his career, death comes and shatters it all. Suddenly, he has to face a world for which he has made no preparation.

Man aims at establishing his own glory on earth, but death comes and demolishes all the delusions of grandeur which he had nurtured, teaching him how powerless he had been before death. Man wants to be his own lord and master, but his helplessness in the hands of fate shows that he has no control over his destiny. Man wants to satisfy his desires in this world, but he is foiled by death, which teaches him to seek in the Hereafter the gratification that constantly eludes him in this world.

We must learn from death, for the secret of life is hidden in the message it has to teach us. Death shows us that we are not our own masters; that our stay on earth is only temporary; that the world is no place for the realization of our dreams. Death teaches us how to live; it shows us the way to real success.

Delusive Grandeur

People usually take worldly success to be an indication of success in the life to come. But they are mistaken in this, for success in this life has nothing to do with eternal success.

Worldly grandeur is no true grandeur at all. It is just a means by which man is put to the test. Some are happily placed in this world, while others are not. But whatever the conditions of human existence, all men are the same in that they are being tested. A person's position on earth is not an indication of success or failure: it is just a test.

When one is raised in stature or in some way honoured in this world, one would be mistaken if one were then to look down on others, for all are equal in the face of death. Death puts the whole human race on one level. Then great are those whom God sees fit to make great, and lowly are those who are cast down by Him.

The world is a place of trial. Here man can pretend to be great, but it will not be long before his real position is exposed. On that day many who have honour in this world will be debased before God; many who claim to be friends of justice and humanity will be exposed as enemies of the very causes they exposed;

many who are acclaimed amongst the brave will be condemned as cowards; many who claimed to bow to the truth will be exposed as shams.

The Inevitable
Fate of Man

The poor are aggrieved by their lowly conditions of living. They eye the rich with envy, not realizing that wealth creates even more problems than poverty. Important figures may appear to command substantial popular support, but in private they have no peace of mind. They are so restless that they cannot sleep at night without the help of sleeping pills. Everyone is beset by problems in this world, though the nature of these problems differs from person to person.

However much happiness one obtains in this life, it can only last for a short time. Death will spare no one. When it comes, wealth and power will be of no avail. Some die walking on the streets, others die while travelling in aeroplanes. Some die in shacks, others in palaces. Death shows no mercy. It is an inevitable fate which everyone has to face.

Death reminds one to look beyond the present, and to seek success beyond this ephemeral world. Those who fail to learn will soon be deprived of the temporary pleasure which they enjoy in this world. They will find themselves in a world of darkness. They will feel remorse at not having prepared themselves for the life after death, but their remorse will not benefit them. They will have to live with their anguish for all time.

Life's Journey

Everyone's mind is full of hopes and ambitions. Everyone cherishes some dream and likes to think that he is progressing towards the fulfillment of that dream. Death puts paid to all his hopes and shows him that he has been travelling towards the world of God, not the world of his own fancies. The journey of his life is not destined to end in this world: he is bound for eternity. How ignorant man is of his own fate! How different from what he imagines his real destination.

Man spends his life ensuring that his children make the most of their future, but he does not live to see the fruits of his efforts. Before long he himself is forced to face a future for which he has made no preparation. Man strives to build himself a comfortable home, but death comes between him and the enjoyment of which he dreamed. Man seeks to enrich himself; he thinks that the more he earns, the more he will advance in honour and prestige. But soon he has to come to terms with the fact that he is bound for the desolation of the grave rather than the honour and prestige of which he dreamed.

Man cannot do without ephemeral comforts. This obsession causes him to deny the stark realities of life. If only he realized that his temporary pleasures would soon be replaced by eternal torment, then his attitude to life would change radically.

God's Mercy

What a shock it will be for man to realize that his activities on earth have come to nothing. People take pride in asserting themselves, but they would do better to take pride in humility. They seek to justify their errors, but they would do better to admit them freely. They have been given tongues with which to praise God, but instead they praise humans. They have been instilled with emotions of love and fear to offer to God, but they waste them on other objects. Hoarding wealth is their greatest aim in life, whereas their greatest aim should be to give their wealth in God's cause. True virtue lies in being kind to the weak, but they ignore the weak and hail the mighty. They would do well to delve into the silent world of meanings, but they prefer to engage in noisy, worthless pursuits.

Progress lies in being able to criticize oneself, but they are busy criticizing others.

Man is living in a fool's paradise of his own making, but the Resurrection will shatter all his dreams. Then, only those who take refuge in His mercy will be saved.

Extraordinary Disillusionment

Man has directed all his efforts towards mundane objects. He is possessed by thoughts of food, clothes, shelter, fame, wealth and happiness. His attention is fixed on the attainment of these worldly goals. He expends all his energy in striving after them. If his efforts are successful, he is pleased. If not, he becomes so discontented that his life is ruined.

Death comes to show man that he is not destined to be happy in this world. Even if one obtains all these things in this world, one can only possess them for a very short time. When, after decades of unremitting struggle, man is at the peak of his powers, death comes and puts paid to his career.

This shows that this world is not meant for the fulfillment of one's hopes and ambitions. The place for their fulfillment is the eternal world in which we are going to dwell after death. People, busy preparing for their worldly future, have neglected their eternal future. They overlook, in the next, more complete life, the very goal which they have set their eyes on this ephemeral world.

Thus man is busy losing exactly what he sets out to gain. What extraordinary disillusionment is in store for him.

The Great Divide

The grave divides this world from the Hereafter. The next world lies across this great divide. Today we are on this side of the divide; tomorrow we will cross it. All living men will taste death; no one will be able to escape it. But man is oblivious of death—the greatest reality of life.

We have all seen people entering the grave never to return, but few of us realize that we are also going to meet the selfsame fate. The door of the grave will open for us and then close on us for ever.

How strange it is that man witnesses others dying every day, but himself lives as if he was never going to die. He can see others being summoned before God every day, but he excludes himself from death's list; he acts as if he was never going to come before the Lord to be judged.

We are closer to death than life. If we could realize this we would look on everyone's death as our own; it would seem as if we ourselves were being carried to the grave when we saw someone else's funeral.

When Words Fail

Every soul shall taste death. Those who see will become sightless and those who speak will be silenced. When death overtakes us, we will leave this world behind and enter the next world. We will leave this world never to return and enter a world in which we will have to abide for ever. We will be removed from the worldly arena of our actions to an arena where we must suffer the eternal consequences of our deeds.

We are closer to death than life. People think they are alive, but it would be truer to say that they are dead, for no one knows when death will come. Death is already upon us. It is not a future event.

Everyone is moving towards death. Some set their eyes on the world, others on eternity; some live for that which meets the eye, others for that which lies beneath the surface. In this world both types of people appear the same but, in relation to their final destination, they are very different. Those who live God-oriented lives are safe, while those who live self-oriented lives are destroying themselves.

The Final Hour

The final hour comes to everyone. It can come while one is sleeping, walking or lying in one's bed. No one can escape this hour, though the form which it takes differs from person to person.

How strange death is. The flame of life is suddenly extinguished; a happy face abruptly fades into oblivion, as if it were less than dust; the aspirations and ambitions that one cherishes on earth are shattered in an instant, as if they were meaningless.

How meaningful life appears, yet its conclusion renders it meaningless. How free man appears to be, yet he is absolutely helpless before death. How dear man's ambitions and desires are to him, but how mercilessly the hand of fate brings them to nothing.

If one only remembers death, one will never be arrogant. The secret of a good life is to stay within one's own bounds: death alone can teach one the truth of this.

Death teaches one not to despise others, for soon one will be brought low oneself. Death reminds one not to crush others, for soon one will be crushed beneath tons of earth oneself.

The Coming Day

Death will surely carry man off. On the day of death the angels will come to take man before his Lord.

It will not be long before man is carried off, but people know only about this happening to others; they do not realize that the same fate awaits them. They gossip about the demise of others, but they forget that one day the angels will also take them before the Lord to be judged.

People are good at finding faults in others, but they would do better to find faults in themselves. They try to save themselves by justifying their actions, but they can only be saved by admitting their faults.

The day when man is taken before God will be the most awesome of days. If one is really aware of what this day means, one's whole life will change. One will live in this world, but one's mind will be focussed on the Hereafter. One will weigh oneself today on the divine scales of justice on which everyone will be placed after death.

One who fears the hand of God will look on everyone's death as if it were his own. When he sees someone being taken to a human court in handcuffs, he will think of his own fate, when he is brought into the Divine Court to be judged by the Lord of the Universe.

Remembering Death

Man has endless words at his disposal in this world; but there will come a time when he will be at a loss for words. There will be no one to listen to what he has to say, no press to print what he writes, and no loudspeaker to announce his words. The fool's paradise which he had constructed for himself in the world will have been razed to the ground. He will look for some respite from anguish and despair, but there will be none.

If only man were to remember death, the things which make him cruel and unjust would become meaningless; he would realize that his actions are leading him towards Hell. Man cannot make use of the wealth which he holds so dear before death comes and severs him from his earnings for all time. If man were to remember this fact, he would not be so obsessed with self-enrichment in this world. People plot the destruction of others, but before they can carry out their plots, death comes between them and their enemies. If one constantly keeps this fact in mind, one will never seek to harm others; one will never plot the downfall of another.

No one is ready to buy a house which is due to be demolished the next day. No one inhabits a city which is about to be devastated by an earthquake. Yet everyone makes the much more serious mistake of ignoring the most severe earthquake which will strike us—death.

Man's Negligence

Old age is a completely new experience for a person. Life loses all its meaning. One sees that one is about to plunge into an unknown world. One longs for a ray of hope at this decisive time; but death catches one unprepared. Suddenly one is robbed of all one's freedom. One enters, a world where one is helpless and forlorn.

Death haunts us all. We tend to forget about it in our youth, but eventually the hand of fate holds sway. When our life on earth has run its course we are taken to a world of darkness—a world in which we will be bewildered and confused, because we had not prepared for it on earth.

In the daytime man knows that night is coming. He organizes his day in accordance with this knowledge. Then, when night falls, he is sure that soon a new day will break. Yet few are conscious of the coming of the Hereafter. Few look forward to life after death as one who travels by day looks forward to the coming night.

Even fewer realize that we will be exposed to the raging fire of Hell after death. Everyone seems to think that death and Hell are for others, not for himself.

𐓷

Man Stands Alone

Death proves that man is alone. In this world, he lives with others. He has family and friends to keep him company and support him. But death will tear him away from all such attachments; it will isolate him from his friends. Death proves that, in this world, man stands alone; he has no friend or helper.

Every day, everywhere, people see this happening. They see others living amongst family and friends in this world. Then suddenly death descends upon them and isolates them from everybody. They find themselves in a pit where there is no one on either side. How strange and striking this event is; but few take heed of the lesson that it teaches.

In this world one has friends to help one at every stage of life; but after death one will be alone in the grave; one will have to contend with the angels alone; one will come before God with no one to support one.

Man thinks that he has everything in this world, but in fact he has nothing. Death comes to convey this reality to man in the most conclusive possible way.

The Deluge
of Eternity

Death is all that divides us from the next world. No one knows when death will come; it might come at any time, breaking the barrier that divides us from eternity, and unleashing the grave realities of eternity upon us like a deluge. No amount of words of force will be of any use then. Man will stand helpless before his Lord. All those who were lost in the splendours of this world and were not prepared to listen to any admonition will be condemned to eternal doom. Only those who reckoned with themselves, before coming to the Lord to be reckoned with, will be saved.

There is no one more ignorant than those who choose to ignore the coming of this day; but their ignorance will not save them. There is no one weaker than those who depend entirely on worldly supports, for these will crumble and fall, leaving one with nothing to depend upon.

Many who seem to be building for themselves are in fact demolishing their own edifices. Many consider themselves superior to others in this world, but will be proved inferior in the next. This will happen when the deluge of eternity engulfs the whole world. On that day, God, together with His angels, will appear.

Everyone will be questioned as to what they have left behind them in the world, and what they have to take with them into the afterlife.

Man's Ignorance

Talking is the easiest thing in the world, and keeping quiet the most difficult. But there will soon come a time when speech will seem to be such a grave matter that one will wish that one had remained silent all one's life; one will wish that one had renounced the power of speech and that one's tongue had been frozen into a perpetual silence.

There is no greater source of temptation in man's body than his tongue, yet it is his tongue that he misuses more than anything: he uses it to deny rather than accept truth; he uses it to utter evil instead of righteous words. People are quite happy with the way they explain themselves in this world. They do not realize that eventually they are not going to have to answer to any human being; they are going to have to answer to God. If they were conscious of this fact, they would prefer to own up to their worldly disgrace rather than pretend to maintain their honour.

This is all because man wrongly considers himself to be his own master. He forgets that, before long, his true Lord and Master will appear, leaving man to languish in his helplessness.

If people knew what was going to happen to them tomorrow, they would cease to derive enjoyment from their present state. Their pride would suddenly change to humility. It is their ignorance of the after-life which has made the world seem too attractive to them.

¿❧

The Trumpet of the Last Day

Those who truly discover God become completely changed people. Outwardly they appear like anyone else, but inwardly they are quite different. They live on a different level from others.

Such people live in the world, but are in the aura of eternity. Everything in this world seems to them to mirror eternity. They catch a glimpse of the splendours of Paradise in the lustre of this ephemeral world, but are reminded of the torment of Hell when their experiences are bitter. Within the framework of this world, they see a picture of eternity. Life conveys to them the message of death.

The true believer is one who sees the world of eternity within the present world. He lives as if the realities of the next, unseen world were present before him. Unbelievers will also see the next world, but this will only be when all veils have been torn asunder by the shrill noise of the trumpet announcing the resurrection of man. Then, all unseen realities will be visible to man. But man's vision will not profit him on that day, for it will be the time for retribution, not the time to give evidence of one's faith in God.

The angel who is to announce the Last Day is ready and waiting with the trumpet in his hand for God to give the order to sound it. This will be a most terrifying time for man. He will want to speak, but will be struck dumb. He will want to walk, but his legs will not carry him.

The Day of Reckoning

The time will come to pass when the whole of creation will be gathered before the Lord. All voices will be silenced except for the voice of God. Only the truth will have any weight on that day. Nothing else will be of any consequence. On that day man will be judged.

Only death divides us from that day. We are all proceeding towards a fate which will bring us either eternal bliss or eternal torment. Every moment that passes is bringing us closer to the fate that is in store for us. We lose one day more in our lives every day the sun sets, and we will never have another chance like the present to prepare for this awesome day. We have only a comparatively short time in this world, but will have to endure the consequences of our life on earth for ever: either bliss or agonizing punishment.

We are soon going to leave this world where we are free to act, and enter another world where we will reap the consequences of our actions; we must examine our lives before this happens. We will all have to stand before God one day. On that day, how fortunate will be those who are included among God's faithful servants, for they will be honoured in heaven. How unfortunate will be those whom God rejects, for they will have nothing to look forward to except eternal torment and disgrace.

§◆

Only One Chance

Man is an immortal being. He passes part of his time on earth and the rest of his time in the hereafter. This world is for actions; in the next world we will reap the consequences of our actions.

The only chance we have to work for the Hereafter is in this world. Afterwards we shall not be able to act: we shall rather have to bear the consequences of our actions. We have very little time on earth. Many who were once among us on earth are now dead and gone.

In the same way we shall be removed one day from the land of the living. Our lives will end and we shall be brought before the Lord.

This life is the first and last chance that we shall have to build an eternal future for ourselves. We have only one life on earth, and it is in this life that we must prove our worth. We are being tried on earth, and this trial is sure to reach a decisive outcome. We shall not be able to escape the consequences of our actions.

Every second that passes is conclusive, for time that has passed can never return. We have only one chance to show our worth; we can either waste it or put it to good use. We have only one life on earth; we can either grow for ourselves a heavenly crop or an infernal one.

Real Success and Failure

Some seem to be successful in this world and others appear to have failed. For this reason people have come to think of success and failure as confined to this world. Heaven and hell have become for them things of this world, not the next.

But this is no more than an illusion. Real success and failure lie in the next life. Many who consider themselves successful in this world will be shocked to find that the reality is far from what they thought. They will discover there who are the losers and who are the winners; they will see who understood the reality of life and who was taken in by mere appearances; they will realize who forged ahead in the race of life and who was left behind; it will be evident who put his talents to the best possible use and who wasted them on the fleeting enjoyments of this world; it will become clear who has attained to true honour and who has been disgraced.

Failure in its true sense is failure in eternity, and likewise true success is success in eternity. Opportunism and expediency earn one honour and status in this world, but they will be of no use in the Hereafter. People who gained worldly honour in this way will find themselves quite unfit for honour in the everlasting world of God. They will be like an old-fashioned, manual worker, who is considered skillful in an agrarian society, but whose skills are of no use in a modern technological age.

The Greatest Earthquake

Earthquakes are a sign of God. When an earthquake strikes, it demolishes all the props which man relies on. It causes mighty stone fortresses to come tumbling down, just as it reduces flimsy wooden huts to matchsticks. It does not distinguish between the strong and the weak. It strikes the mighty in the same way as it strikes the helpless.

Earthquakes give us prior warning of what is eventually going to happen to all of us in this world. They remind us in this world of the doomsday which all mankind must face in the next world. When the trembling of the earth makes people lose their senses; when houses start falling as if they were made of playing cards; when the earth is turned upside down; then people will realize how utterly helpless they are before the might of God. All man can do at such a time is helplessly gaze on his own destruction.

The earthquake of the Last Day will be infinitely more severe than any worldly earthquake. All man's supports will collapse. He will forget the skills which he displayed in the world. The grandeur which he enjoyed on earth will disappear. The only people who will have anything to rely on will be those who did not rely on worldly supports. The successful one on that day will be those who attached themselves to God, while others had taken refuge under other banners.

On the Verge of Death

Everyone is on the move and everyone's journey ends in death. Death means heaven for some and hell for others. Fortunate are those who find themselves on the threshold of heaven at the time of death; they will dwell in eternal bliss; they will know neither grief nor apprehension. But there is no limit to the misfortune of those whom death brings to the threshold of hell; for they will be trapped forever in a world of fire and smoke.

Those who acknowledge God's greatness and bow before Him, who abide by the truth and do good to others, are the ones who will be admitted into heaven.

Those who do not acknowledge the greatness of God, who are unjust in their dealing with others, who are cruel and proud towards their fellows, will be condemned to Hell.

Heaven is for those who are of a heavenly nature in this world, while Hell is for those who do not make their lives conform to heavenly standards.

All too Soon

Man seeks wealth, honour, power and offspring in this world. He does all he can to obtain these things, but death shows him that his desires cannot be fulfilled in this world. He cannot find in this ephemeral world what he longs for above all else.

One only has to think: what is the point of gaining anything in this world when one is bound to leave it behind in a few days? If one were to be content with one's lot in this world, all the plundering and exploitation that man indulges in would then cease. It is a fact that there is no great difference between acquiring a thing and not acquiring it: what is the value of an acquisition which the very next day is going to be turned to loss? Man expends all his energies to obtain something, only to lose it the next moment. Life is sure to end in death. Man will leave behind all the valued possessions which he surrounds himself with in this world, never to return to them again.

Man lives for today; he forgets about tomorrow. He builds a home for himself by destroying others' homes, although tomorrow he is going to step into the grave. He takes others to human courts, where he makes out false cases against them; he forgets that the angels are standing over him, ready to take him to the divine court. He looks down on others, thinking he is secure in his worldly greatness, but this greatness will soon be destroyed, and there will be no trace of it left.

Divine Scales of Justice

In this world of trial every man is free. It is possible to torment one's neighbour, yet still be acclaimed for one's piety. One may be struggling for leadership, yet still be hailed as a holy crusader. One may choose to be unjust to those one deals with, yet still be invited to preside over meetings whose aim is to promote peace and justice. One may be forgetful of God in private, yet in public places, be considered a representative of the divine cause. One may be totally indifferent to the plight of the oppressed, yet still find a place in the headlines as friend of the downtrodden. One may only be spouting empty words, yet be given credit for beneficent actions.

No facade, however perfect, can conceal man's true nature from God. But he keeps his superior knowledge hidden in this world and will reveal it only in the hereafter. The scales of God will be put into place and everyone will be seen for what he is. There is no doubting the coming of that day. No one will be able to postpone it or escape from it. Wise are they who prepare for that day by placing themselves today on the divine scales of justice; for those who are placed on them tomorrow will be damned.

After Death

All men will have to face death sooner or later. They will leave the world behind them never to return. Ahead of them will be the Hereafter. They will have no option but to enter this new world.

The Judgement Day is approaching fast. On that day every soul will appear as it really was. All the veils that conceal a person's true nature in the world will disappear. Beautiful words will be of no avail in concealing that true nature.

In this world a selfish person can appear as a godly one. One who is hungry for fame can present himself before men as a standard-bearer of truth. One who places self-interest before all in his work can by clever talk deceive people into thinking that he is selflessly serving the cause of truth.

But death is the event in man's life that exposes all such pretence as false. In the world after death all such veils will disappear. Man will appear as he really is for himself and for others as well.

Brought Before God

Death is not the end of our lives; it is the beginning of our real life. After death man will be brought before the Lord for final judgement.

Man has many concerns in this world, but after death he will be concerned with one thing alone: escaping from the wrath of God. If one has ample time at one's disposal, one engages in many tasks. But if time is short then one concentrates on the most important task. At crucial moments, no one is foolhardy enough to engage in irrelevant pursuits.

No time is fixed for death. It can come at any moment. This fact makes death an even more delicate issue. First and foremost, we should communicate to others the dangers that death holds in store for us; we should inform people about tomorrow, before it is upon us.

This is the essence of the message of Islam. Islam calls man to faith in the Hereafter; it seeks to awake the living to the issues that will face the dead. The preacher of Islam stands between life and death. While still on earth, it is as if he has already experienced death and is thus able to inform his fellows of what lies beyond the grave.

The Greatest Calamity

The greatest calamity afflicting our world is that one million people die every day. No one knows, of those who are alive today, who will be dead tomorrow. Every one of us shall taste death, but no one knows when death will come. We do not know which of our fellow men will leave this world tomorrow, and who will remain to receive this message.

Every one of us is hastening towards this fate. Everyone who is alive today is in danger of dying tomorrow. Then we will not have the chance to warn others, nor they the chance to listen.

Under these circumstances, it is clear what our real task must be: we must dwell on the life after death and warn our fellows of it, for this is the real issue of life. There are over four billion people on earth, and this task applies to each and every one of them. Everyone is ignorant of the reality of life, and everyone needs to be informed of it. If a strong hurricane is approaching, one forgets trivial matters. Death is greater than a hurricane. If one were to realize this, one would think and speak about death more than anything.

Warning People of the Hereafter

Muslims have a responsibility to God: to tell all nations of the world that the day shall come when God will judge them, meting out reward and punishment according to the merits and demerits of people's actions. The Muslims' present and future well-being rests entirely upon their fulfillment of this responsibility. Their value lies in the performance of this service of conveying the divine message. They are of no value in the sight of God if they do not rise to this task.

If Muslims neglect this responsibility, nothing that they do will be acceptable to God; even their apparently religious work will count for nothing. When they neglect this responsibility, God will leave them to their enemies; He will set other nations over them. Even the movements, which they call Islamic, but which are not aimed at the execution of this duty, will come to nothing. They will continue to indulge in wishful thinking, but they will not be able to deny the truth of the fact that God has deserted them.

If Muslims do not rise to the task of warning people of the next life, they lose their worth in the sight of God; they become disgraced and miserable both in this world and the next. One only has to look at the vicissitudes in the history of the Jewish people to understand this fact. Man's worth is in relation to his performance of the duties which have been entrusted to him. If Muslims neglect their duty to God, then how will they be of any worth in His sight?

Responsibility of Preaching

In this world, floods come to remind us of a greater flood which will come in the Hereafter. Every year, in some part of the globe, towns and villages are submerged in flood waters. The day when man rises from the dead, there will be a huge flood of this nature. All protective measures will disintegrate before the oncoming flood. It will submerge all of us; even high mountains will not be able to give us safe harbour.

The ones who survive worldly floods are those who have prepared boats before the coming of the flood. So, the survivors of the great flood of the Hereafter will be those who ride in God's boat by giving themselves up to Him.

Mankind must be warned of the flood that is descending upon him. To issue this warning is the greatest task in the world today. It was to warn mankind of the coming of this flood that God sent His messengers to the world; so that after death, when man is brought before God, no one will be able to claim ignorance, and say that he is being punished for something he had never been told about.

No prophet will come to the world now, but this task is still as important as ever. After the termination of prophethood, this special mission of the Prophet has been entrusted to the followers of the final Prophet. They must fulfill their duty, before God unleashes the flood waters upon us, or no one will have a chance to warn others, or be warned himself.

The Awe-Inspiring Day of Retribution

What an awe-inspiring day it will be when God sits in judgement. No one will be able to be defiant or proud. Those who had been considered worthless and rejected in the world will be raised in value and accepted in God's sight. Those who had been considered weakest among men will, by the grace of God, be given great importance: it will be according to their testimony that people will be sent either to heaven or to Hell.

Those who were loquacious in the world will be rejected by God. Those who were thought of as mighty and powerful in the world will be reduced to powerlessness. Those who feigned piety in the world will be exposed for the impious beings they really were. Their brightness will be dimmed and, for them, white will be turned into black.

People are hidden behind artificial appearances in this world. Some hide themselves behind seductive words; others conceal their true natures behind material grandeur and splendour. But they will be denied these things in the life to come. Everyone will appear in his true garb. One who realizes the awe-inspiring nature of that day will suddenly be reduced to silence; worldly honour will seem to him as meaningless as worldly disgrace.

The Soul of Islam

The true believer is one who actually sees the Archangel Israfil standing, waiting to sound the trumpet which will signal the end of the world. This is the true difference between a believer and a disbeliever; the disbeliever lives for this world, while the believer lives for the next world; the disbeliever is engrossed in the outward form of life, while the believer discovers the inner truth of life in its final outcome.

Islam means to devote one's life entirely to God. A

243

man's soul should commune with God in this world. If this is not the case, it means that the true spirit of religion is lacking. People may claim to believe in God, but their belief consists of an attachment to empty rituals. They bring religion down to the level of their own consciousness, and neglect the spirit of true submission to God.

When this happens, people tend to ignore the spirit behind religious observances, and as a result, only outward forms survive. People stop crying to the Lord in private, they are interested only in public espousal of 'Islamic' causes. Mosques are crowded by worshippers but the prayers do not succeed in illuminating their souls. People do not concentrate on abstinence in fasting, but rather on having lavish meals before and after the fast. The spirit of servitude is lacking in religious festivals, which become instead occasions for self-indulgent, ostentatious enjoyment. The Prophet's life ceases to be an example for his followers; instead they show their attachment to the Prophet by celebrating his anniversary and holding conventions in his honour.

In short, when the spirit is lacking, religion is moulded in the form of the worldliness of its adherents.

Hushed Silence
Among the Crowd

When religion becomes part of a national tradition, a new phenomenon comes into existence: ceremonies performed in the name of religion increase, but true religion disappears entirely.

This is what is happening to the Muslims today. The number of people who pray is on the increase, but there are few who really fear God. There is no lack of people who will speak on behalf of Islam, but there are few who will remain silent for the sake of their religion. Everybody sees his own righteousness, but few see righteousness in others. There are plenty who are ready to display their piety in public, but few are really pious in private. Everyone wants to see Islam established in the whole world, but no one has time to establish it in the individual self. Everybody has huge reserves of fine words at his disposal, but few have any fine actions to offer. Everybody thinks he has the key to paradise, but few feel the need to tremble in fear of Hell. Everybody is enthusiastic about Islam when it is embellished with material grandeur, but no one is interested in the Islam which shakes one's soul and makes one live in awareness of the afterlife.

Never before in the midst of such a proliferation of religious activities has there been such spiritual bankruptcy.

Tell Me About HAJJ
What the Hajj Is, Why It's So Important and What It Teaches Me

SANIYASNAIN KHAN

Tell Me About THE PROPHET MUHAMMAD
What the Prophet's Message Is, Why His Life Is So Important and What He Teaches Me

SANIYASNAIN KHAN

Tell Me About THE PROPHET MUSA
What the Prophet's Message Is, Why His Life Is So Important and What He Teaches Me

SANIYASNAIN KHAN

THE **MIRACLE IN THE ANT**
HARUN YAHYA

THE SERIES OF FACTS DEMOLISHING THE LIE OF EVOLUTION - 3

ALLAH IS KNOWN THROUGH REASON

HARUN YAHYA

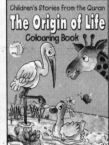

Children's Stories from the Quran
The Origin of Life Colouring Book

LIFE BEGINS
Quran Stories for Little Hearts

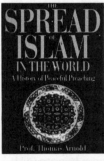

THE **SPREAD OF ISLAM IN THE WORLD**
A History of Peaceful Preaching

Prof. Thomas Arnold

Islamic Medicine

EDWARD G. BROWNE

Islamic Thought and its Place in History

De Lacy O'Leary

ISLAM **REDISCOVERED**
Discovering Islam from its Original Sources

MAULANA WAHIDUDDIN KHAN

THE **ISLAMIC ART AND ARCHITECTURE**
SIR THOMAS ARNOLD

DECISIVE MOMENTS IN THE HISTORY OF ISLAM

MUHAMMAD ABDULLAH ENAN

A **HAND BOOK OF MUSLIM BELIEF**
DR. AHMAD A GALWASH

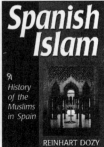

Spanish Islam
A History of the Muslims in Spain

REINHART DOZY

Goodword Books

Tell Me About the Prophet Muhammad (HB)
Tell Me About the Prophet Muhammad (PB)
Tell Me About the Prophet Musa (HB)
Tell Me About Hajj (HB)
Tell Me About Hajj (PB)
Honeybees that Build Perfect Combs
The World of Our Little Friends, the Ants
Life Begins (PB)
The First Man (HB)
The First Man (PB)
The Two Brothers (HB)
The Two Brothers (PB)
The Ark of Nuh (HB)
The Ark of Nuh (PB)
The Brave Boy (PB)
Allah's Best Friend (PB)
The Travels of the Prophet Ibrahim
The Origin of Life (Colouring Book)
The First Man on the Earth (Colouring Book)
The Two Sons of Adam (Colouring Book)
The Ark of Nuh and the Animals (Colouring Book)
The Brave Boy (Colouring Book)
Allah's Best Friend (Colouring Book)
The Travels of the Prophet Ibrahim (Colouring Book)
The Ark of Nuh and the Great Flood (Sticker Book)
The Story of the Prophet Nuh (HB)
The Story of the Prophet Nuh (PB)
The Blessings of Ramadan (PB)
The Story of Prophet Yusuf
Stories from the Quran
The Holy Mosques
The Holy Quran (PB)
The Holy Quran (Laminated Board)
The Holy Quran (HB)

A Dictionary of Muslim Names
The Most Beautiful Names of Allah (HB)
The Most Beautiful Names of Allah (PB)
The Pilgrimage to Makkah
One Religion
Islamic Economics
The Story of Islamic Spain (PB)
The Travels of Ibn Battuta
Humayun Nama
Islamic Sciences
Islamic Thought...
The Qur'an for Astronomy
Arabic-English Dictionary for Advanced Learners
The Spread of Islam in the World
A Handbook of Muslim Belief
The Muslims in Spain
The Moriscos of Spain
Spanish Islam (A History of the Muslims in Spain)
A Simple Guide to Muslim Prayer
A Simple Guide to Islam
A Simple Guide to Islam's Contribution to Science
The Quran, Bible and Science
Islamic Medicine
Islam and the Divine Comedy
The Travels of Ibn Jubayr
The Arabs in History
Decisive Moments in the History of Islam
My Discovery of Islam
Islam At the Crossroads
The Spread of Islam in France
The Islamic Art and Architecture
The Islamic Art of Persia
The Hadith for Beginners
How Greek Science Passed to Arabs
Islamic Thought and its Place in History
Muhammad: The Hero As Prophet
A History of Arabian Music
A History of Arabic Literature

The Quran
Selections from the Noble Reading
The Koran
Allah is Known Through Reason
The Miracle in the Ant
The Miracle in the Immune System
The Miracle of Creation in Plants
The Miracle in the Spider
Eternity Has Already Begun
Timelessness and the Reality of Fate
Ever Thought About the Truth?
Crude Understanding of Disbelief
Quick Grasp of Faith
Death Resurrection Hell
The Basic Concepts in the Quran
The Moral Values of the Quran
Heart of the Koran
Muhammad: A Mercy to All the Nations
The Sayings of Muhammad
The Beautiful Commands of Allah
The Beautiful Promises of Allah
The Muslim Prayer Encyclopaedia
After Death, Life!
Living Islam: Treading the Path of Ideal
A Basic Dictionary of Islam
The Muslim Marriage Guide
GCSE Islam—The Do-It-Yourself Guide
The Soul of the Quran
Presenting the Quran
The Wonderful Universe of Allah
The Life of the Prophet Muhammad
History of the Prophet Muhammad
A-Z Steps to Leadership
The Essential Arabic
A Case of Discovery